Painted Pots

Painted
Pots

Sterling Publishing Co., Inc. New York
A Sterling / Chapelle Book

Chapelle, Ltd.:
- Owner: Jo Packham
- Editor: Laura Best
- Staff: Marie Barber, Ann Bear, Areta Bingham, Kass Burchett, Rebecca Christensen, Holly Fuller, Marilyn Goff, Shirley Heslop, Holly Hollingsworth, Shawn Hsu, Susan Jorgensen, Leslie Liechty, Pauline Locke, Barbara Milburn, Linda Orton, Karmen Quinney, Rhonda Rainey, Leslie Ridenour, Cindy Stoeckl

Plaid Enterprises:
- Editor: Mickey Baskett
- Staff: Jeff Herr, Laney McClure, Susan Mickey, Dianne Miller, Jerry Mucklow, Phyllis Mueller, and Susanne Yoder

If you have any questions or comments or would like information on specialty products featured in this book, please contact Chapelle, Ltd., Inc., P.O. Box 9252, Ogden, UT 84409 • (801) 621-2777 • (801) 621-2788 Fax

Due to the limited amount of space available, we must print our patterns at a reduced size in order to give our patrons the maximum number of patterns possible in our publications. We believe the quality and quantity of our patterns will compensate for any inconvenience this may cause.

Library of Congress Cataloging-in-Publication Data

Painted pots / Plaid.
       p.   cm.
"Sterling/Chapelle Book"
   includes index.
   ISBN 0-8069-8155-5
     1. Painting.   2. Decoration and ornament.   3. Flowerpots.
  I. Plaid Enterprises.
TT385.p36   1998
745.7'23—de21   98-20970
                            CIP

A Sterling/Chapelle Book

10 9 8 7 6 5 4

First paperback edition published in 1999 by
Sterling Publishing Company, Inc.
387 Park Avenue South, New York, N.Y. 10016
Produced by Chapelle Ltd.
P.O. Box 9252, Newgate Station, Ogden, Utah 84409
© 1998 by Chapelle Ltd.
Distributed in Canada by Sterling Publishing
% Canadian Manda Group, One Atlantic Avenue, Suite 105
Toronto, Ontario, Canada M6K 3E7
Distributed in Great Britain and Europe by Cassell PLC
Wellington House, 125 Strand, London WC2R 0BB, England
Distributed in Australia by Capricorn Link (Australia) Pty, Ltd.
P.O. Box 704, Windsor, NSW 2756 Australia
Printed in China
All rights reserved

Sterling ISBN 0-8069-8155-5 Trade
             0-8069-8201-2 Paper

Contents

Contents

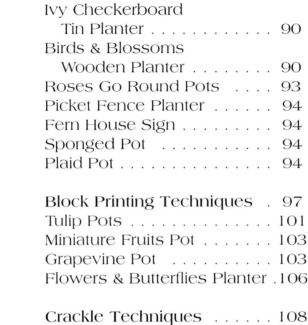

Introduction

Flower pots are versatile and useful containers making wonderful centerpieces and seasonal decorations.

With a liner to hold a cake or colorful napkins, pots can be used as serving dishes for themed buffets, or used to hold kitchen utensils, pens and pencils, fruits and vegetables — even plants!

Decorated flower pots are wonderful containers for all kinds of gifts — bath items and toiletries, flower bulbs, candies, and candles.

This book contains instructions for decorating more than 50 flower pot and garden-themed projects. With the talents of a number of creative designers, various techniques of decorative painting, stenciling, block printing, découpage, crackling, antiquing, sponging, and dimensional painted designs are explained.

Projects for containers that can be used to hold plants, such as planters and boxes, are included. The flower pot motif also is used to decorate a variety of wood, metal, and papîer maché items for home and garden. Complete patterns are included.

Through beautiful photographs, easy to follow instructions, and techniques, this book is a valuable reference you will return to often. You will also learn about the types of products used to create these projects, which are available at hardware, crafts, and building supply stores.

SUPPLIES YOU WILL NEED

Acrylic Craft Paints:

Acrylic craft paints are premixed, richly pigmented, flat finish paints that come ready to use. These high-quality paints are available in a huge range of colors, including rich metallics.

These paints can be used to base-coat surfaces before painting designs, as well as to do the actual design painting.

Acrylic Gloss Enamels:

Acrylic gloss enamels are weather resistant and durable. They can be used indoors or outdoors. Their bright, intense colors allow for an opaque coverage. There are also high-quality acrylic craft paints in a gloss enamel formulation, which dry to a gloss finish and can be used outdoors without a protective finish.

Acrylic Painting Mediums:

Acrylic painting mediums are used with paint to create certain effects or change the paint's performance. Some mediums are mixed with paint before application; others are applied to surfaces before painting.

Blending Gel Mediums:

Blending gel mediums are applied to surfaces before painting to increase drying time and make it easier to smoothly blend colors.

Extenders:

Extenders are used to increase drying time. They become transparent when floating, blending, and washing colors.

Floating Mediums:

Floating mediums are used instead of water for floating, shading, and highlighting. Since floating mediums do not run like water, they offer more control.

- Angular shaders are used for floating.

- Fan brushes are used for a whispy coverage.

- Mop brushes are used for blending and softening.

- Deerfoot brushes or old flat brushes are used for stippling.

- Scruffy brushes are old, worn out flat brushes used for stippling and dry brushing.

- Sponge brushes are used for base-coating.

Aerosol Finishes:

Aerosol finishes are sprayed onto painted surfaces to seal and protect against moisture, soil, and dust. They dry clear and are non-yellowing. Finishes are available in satin, matte, or gloss. Choose the amount of shine desired or use the finish specified in the individual project instructions.

Waterbase Varnishes:

Waterbase varnishes are brushed onto surfaces to seal and protect against moisture, soil, and dust. They dry with a satin finish. They offer excellent resistance to scratches and water spotting.

Brushes:

Brush quality is important to the success of painting. Quality brushes bend easily, then return to their original shape. Use the best quality brush you can afford.

There are no set rules for choosing brushes. Try a variety of styles and qualities to make your choice.

Brushes are made from either synthetics or animal hair. Synthetic brushes are made especially for use with acrylic paints. Brushes are designed for specific purposes:

- Liners and script liners are used for small details and lettering. Script liners hold more paint for long, continuous strokes.

- Scrollers are used for fine detailing.

- Round brushes are used for delicate lines and detail work. Round brushes have a fine point. The size of the brush to be used is determined by the size of the detail to be painted.

- Flat brushes are used for base-coating, sideloading, and floating. Flat brushes have long hairs and a chisel edge. The size of the brush to be used is determined by the size of the detail to be painted.

- Filbert brushes are used for strokes with soft edges.

Brush Care:

Cleaning brushes after each use is extremely important. Rinse bristles in water, then clean with a good brush cleaner. Rinse and reshape wet bristles. Flat brushes should have a fine, chiseled edge; round brushes and liners should come to a very fine point. Let dry. Before painting again, rinse bristles.

Other Supplies:

- Art erasers are used for removing pattern lines.

- Brush cleaners are used for cleaning and conditioning brushes.

- Disposable plates are used as palettes for arranging and mixing paints.

- Palette knives are used for mixing paints.

- Paper towels are used for wiping brushes and cleanup.

- Sandpaper is used for removing burrs and rough spots from wood.

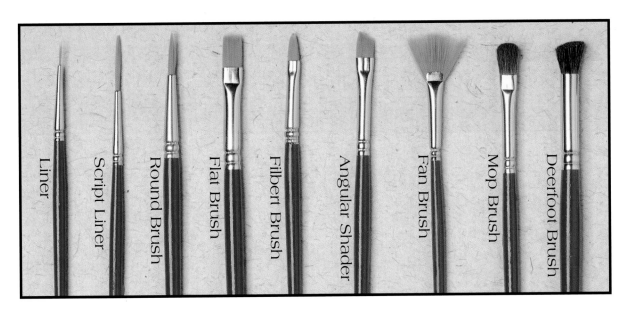

Liner Script Liner Round Brush Flat Brush Filbert Brush Angular Shader Fan Brush Mop Brush Deerfoot Brush

• Styluses are used for transferring patterns to surfaces.

• Tack cloth is used for removing sanding dust from wood.

• Transfer tools, such as a stylus, pencil, and/or tracing paper, are used for tracing and transfering patterns onto projects.

• Water basins are used for rinsing brushes.

(See individual project instructions for additional supplies needed.)

HOW TO USE THIS BOOK

• Read through instructions before beginning a painting project. Paint project steps in order specified. Always keep instructions and project photographs handy while working.

• Practice a few strokes before attempting the project. Place tracing paper or plastic over painting worksheet.

Practice painting the stroke on the overlay. Practicing strokes will improve your painting.

• Project patterns are included in this book. Photocopy them, enlarging or reducing as needed to fit your painting surface, or trace them on tracing paper. To transfer, position photocopied or traced design on project surface. Secure with tape. Slip transfer paper, between pattern and project surface. With a transfer tool, retrace pattern lines. Use enough pressure to transfer lines without denting surface.

SURFACE PREPARATION

Preparing Clay Pots:
    Most projects are painted on clay pots and saucers, available at garden centers and hardware stores.
    Sand rough areas on pots and saucers with extra-fine (220 grit) sandpaper or a sanding sponge. Wipe away dust and be certain all areas are clean and dry. Using a sponge brush or large flat

brush, base-coat with color specified. Let dry. Apply a second coat.
    If painting directly inside pot, it will first need to be sealed on the inside and outside to waterproof. If this precaution is not taken, moisture seeping through the terracotta will ruin the painting. Using an acrylic sealer, brush it on both sides and let dry before base-coating the pot.
    It is not necessary to plant directly in a pot. Instead, use the decorated pot as a cache pot, and use a slightly smaller clay or plastic pot inside decorated pot to hold plant.

Preparing Unfinished Wood:
    Sand new wood with medium (150 grit) sandpaper in the direction of the grain. Wipe away dust with a tack cloth or a soft cloth. (If planting directly in a wooden planter, seal both inside and outside of wood. Let dry.)
    Using a large, flat brush, base-coat with color specified, making smooth, even strokes. Let dry. Sand lightly. Apply second coat of paint. Let dry.

Option: Base-coat, let dry, sand, and wipe clean. Apply matte sealer spray.

Preparing Painted Wood:

Sand painted wood with medium (150 grit) sandpaper until surface feels smooth. Wipe away paint particles with a tack cloth or soft cloth. It is not necessary to remove all the old paint.

Preparing New Tin:

Wash new tin with a mixture of equal parts of vinegar and water. Let dry. Using steel wool, rub tin. Wipe with a tack cloth. Base-coat according to individual project instructions.

Preparing Old Tin:

Using steel wool, rub tin. Wipe with a tack cloth. Base-coat according to individual project instructions.

Preparing Papîer Maché:

Papîer maché pieces are decorative and are not meant for outdoor use.

No preparation is required. The surface can be painted, antiqued, faux finished, découpaged, or textured. The smooth surface allows the brush to glide easily and slight surface irregularities add interest.

Using a large, flat brush, base-coat with color specified, making smooth, even strokes. Let dry. Apply as many coats as necessary, letting each coat dry.

After painting, apply matte spray sealer and let dry.

Papîer maché does not have to be base-coated—the design can be painted directly onto papîer maché surface.

PAINTING TIPS

Working with Acrylics:
• Squeeze paint onto palette, making a puddle of paint about the size of a nickel.

• Pull color with brush from edge of puddle. Do not dip brush in center of puddle; putting too much paint on edges.

• Let each coat dry before applying a second coat. If an area is cool to the touch, it is probably still wet.

• Acrylic paints blend easily. Add white to lighten a color. Add black to darken.

BASIC PAINTING TERMS

Base-coat:
Cover an entire area with one initial coat. Shade and highlight on top of base coat.

Double-load:
Load two colors, one on each half of the brush. When reloading, keep same color on same half of brush each time.

Highlight:
Add dimension by adding colors. Load brush with extender, sideload with highlight color, and apply to design.

Inky:
Mix paint with water until paint is the consitency of ink.

Load:
Stroke brush back and forth in paint until brush is full.

Shade:
Shading creates shadows, darkens and deepens color, and makes an area recede.

Load brush with extender or floating medium, sideload with shading color, and apply to design.

Sideload:
Sideload when shading or highlighting. Load brush, picking up another color for shading on one edge of brush. When sideloading for floating, dip a flat brush in water and blot once on a paper towel. Load only left corner of brush with paint. Stroke brush back and forth on palette until paint gradually blends into water.

Spatter:
Using an old toothbrush or stencil brush, dip bristles into water. Blot on a paper towel to remove excess water. Dip brush into paint, working paint into bristles by tapping on palette. Point brush toward area to be spattered and pull thumb across bristles.

Undercoat:
Undercoat part of design with white paint when painting on a dark surface, so design paint color shows.

Wash:
Using four parts paint to one part water, load brush and use long strokes to make a transparent layer of paint over a base color.

Wet on Wet:
While paint is still wet, pick up shading or highlighting color on brush and paint area, blending new color into previous one.

Simple Brush Strokes

Undercoat shape in white to make base coat more brilliant.

Base-coat design shape by filling in solidly with color.

Load brush by pulling color away from edge of puddle.

Load liner with extender. Dip into paint. Blend on palette until thin consistency.

Sideload flat brush with extender. Load tip of side with paint.

Blend sideloaded brush on palette.

Double-load flat brush by loading color to each side. Blend on palette before painting.

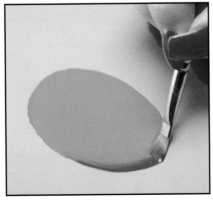

Shade by sideloading with a darker color.

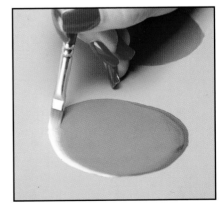

Highlight by sideloading with a lighter color.

Comma stroke, using flat brush

S-stroke, using flat brush

Comma stroke start, using round brush

Comma stroke end, using round brush

Curved lines, using script liner

Straight lines, using liner

Ruffles, using angular brush

Petals, using angular brush

Flat Brush

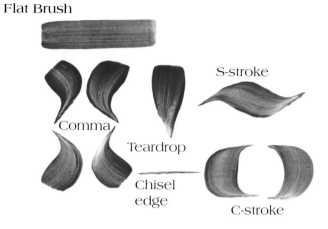

Comma

S-stroke

Teardrop

Chisel edge

C-stroke

Round Brush

Comma

Scroll

Teardrop

Flower petals

Liner and Script Liner

Angular Brush

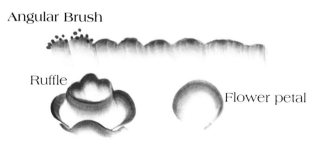

Ruffle

Flower petal

Starting comma stroke, using filbert brush

Ending comma stroke, using filbert brush

Patting motion, using deerfoot brush

Making grass, using deerfoot brush

Making hearts, using brush handle

Blending or softening color, using mop brush

Making checkerboards, using square sponge

Pouncing surface, using square sponge

Filbert

Stencil Brush

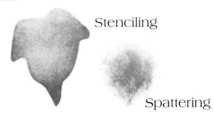

Stenciling

Spattering

Deerfoot Brush

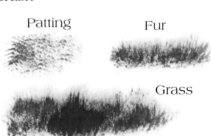

Patting

Fur

Grass

Mop Brush

Softening edges or blending

Handle End of Brush

Dots

Dot heart

Dot flower

Sponge

Square

Checkerboard

13

**Green Striped
Pot with
White Rim**
Instructions begin
on page 16

**Two-toned
Striped Pot**
Instructions begin
on page 16

Faith, Hope,
Love & Charity Pot
Instructions begin
on page 16

Green & Pink
Striped Pot
Instructions begin
on page 17

Green Striped Pot with White Rim

Pictured on page 14

Designed by
Susan Driggers

GATHER THESE SUPPLIES

Painting Surface:
Clay pot with lip, 4" dia.

Paints, Stains, and Finishes:
Acrylic craft paints:
    Alizarian Crimson
    Brilliant Blue
    Hunter Green
    Mystic Green
    Wicker White
Glazing medium
Matte spray sealer

Brushes:
Flat brush, #12
Liner, #00

Other Supplies:
Masking tape, ½" wide
Ruler

INSTRUCTIONS

Prepare:
1. See Surface Preparation on page 9. Prepare clay pot.

Paint the Design:
1. Using a #12 flat brush, base-coat pot with Mystic Green.

2. Mix Wicker White with equal part glazing medium. Wash pot with mixture.

3. Paint top lip with Wicker White. Let dry.

4. Place masking tape around rim ¼" from bottom.

5. Mix Hunter Green with glazing medium, two parts medium to one part paint. Using a #12 flat brush, paint a horizontal stripe between masking tape and bottom of rim. Let dry. Remove tape.

6. Place vertical strips of masking tape ½" apart to form stripes. Paint stripes around lower part of pot. Let dry. Remove tape.

7. Using a #00 liner, paint a thin stripe of Alizarian Crimson to right of each vertical Hunter Green stripe.

8. Mix Brilliant Blue with glazing medium, two parts medium to one part paint. Paint a ¼" wide stripe to the right of each Alizarian Crimson stripe. Let dry.

Finish:
1. Apply matte spray sealer.

Two-tone Striped Pot

Pictured on page 14

Designed by
Susan Driggers

GATHER THESE SUPPLIES

Painting Surface:
Clay pot, 5" dia.
Clay saucer, 4½" dia.

Paints, Stains, and Finishes:
Acrylic craft paints:
    Burnt Sienna
    Linen
Matte spray sealer

Brushes:
Flat brush, #12

Other Supplies:
Masking tape, ¾" wide
Ruler

INSTRUCTIONS

Prepare:
1. See Surface Preparation on page 9. Prepare clay pot.

Paint the Design:
1. Using a #12 flat brush, base-coat bottom of pot and saucer with Linen. Let dry.

2. Place vertical strips of masking tape ¾" apart to form stripes.

3. Paint stripes and rims of pot and saucer with Burnt Sienna. Let dry. Remove tape.

Finish:
1. Apply matte spray sealer.

Faith, Hope, Love & Charity Pot

Pictured on page 15

Designed by
Susan Driggers

GATHER THESE SUPPLIES

Painting Surface:
Clay pot, 7" dia.
Clay saucer, 5½" dia.

Paints, Stains, and Finishes:
Acrylic craft paints:
    Burnt Sienna
    Burnt Umber
    Butter Pecan
    Hunter Green
    Linen
Matte spray sealer

Brushes:
Flat brushes, #12, ¾"
Liner, #00
Old toothbrush

Other Supplies:
Masking tape, 1" wide
Newspaper
Ruler

INSTRUCTIONS

Prepare:
1. See Surface Preparation on page 9. Prepare clay pot.

Paint the Design:
1. Using a #12 flat brush, base-coat pot and saucer with Linen. Let dry.

2. Place masking tape strips 1" apart forming vertical stripes. Using a ¾" flat brush, lightly paint stripes with Hunter Green. Let dry. Remove tape.

3. Paint a narrow stripe with Burnt Sienna to the right of each Hunter Green stripe.

4. Paint a stripe ½" wide with Butter Pecan to the right of each Burnt Sienna stripe.

5. Protect stripes with newspaper. Dilute Burnt Sienna with mixture of two parts water to one part paint.

6. Using an old toothbrush, spatter rims of pot and saucer with diluted Burnt Sienna.

7. Using a #00 liner and the Striped Pots Lettering below as an example, paint words: L'amour, Le foi, and L'espérance around rim of pot with Burnt Umber. Let dry.

Finish:
1. Apply matte spray sealer.

Green & Pink Striped Pot

Pictured on page 15

Designed by
Susan Driggers

GATHER THESE SUPPLIES

Painting Surface:
Clay pot, 4" dia.

Paints, Stains, and Finishes:
Acrylic craft paints:
    Basil Green
    Clover
    Raspberry Sherbet
Matte spray sealer

Brush:
Flat brush, #12
Liner, #00

Other Supplies:
Masking tape, ⅞" wide
Ruler

INSTRUCTIONS

Prepare:
1. See Surface Preparation on page 9. Prepare clay pot.

Paint the Design:
1. Using a #12 flat brush, base-coat pot with Basil Green. Let dry.

2. Place masking tape around pot, ¾" from bottom, and around top and bottom of rim to make a stripe 1¼" wide. Paint a stripe around rim and bottom of pot with Raspberry Sherbet. Let dry. Remove tape.

3. Place vertical strips of tape around rim of pot, ¾" apart to form stripes. Paint between strips with Clover.

4. Paint inside of pot with Clover. Using a #00 liner, paint narrow vertical stripes around bottom of pot with Clover. Let dry. Remove tape.

5. Using the Striped Pots Lettering below as an example, paint words: Le Rose, La fleur, Les fleurs around bottom of pot with Clover. Let dry.

Finish:
1. Apply matte spray sealer.

Striped Pots Lettering

L'amour   Le foi   L'espérance
Le Rose • La fleur • Les fleurs

Potting Bench
Instructions begin on page 19

Potting Bench

Pictured on page 18

Designed by
Chris Stokes

GATHER THESE SUPPLIES

Painting Surface:
Wooden bench,
   30" x 11" x 16" high

Paints, Stains, and Finishes:
Acrylic craft paints:
   Burnt Sienna
   Burnt Umber
   Emerald Isle
   Fresh Foliage
   Licorice
   Light Red Oxide
   Magenta
   Tapioca
   True Blue
   Wicker White
   Yellow Light
Antiquing medium:
   Down Home Brown
Waterbase varnish

Brushes:
Flat brushes, #2, #10
Old toothbrush
Stencil brush

Other Supplies:
Paper towel
Sponge, ½" square
   compressed
Transfer tool

INSTRUCTIONS

Prepare:
1. See Surface Preparation on pages 9-10. Prepare wooden bench.

2. Antique entire bench with Down Home Brown. Let dry.

3. Using a #10 flat brush, base-coat top, front, and back pieces with Tapioca. Let dry.

4. Dampen compressed sponge. Squeeze out excess water. Dip sponge in Licorice and sponge checkerboard squares on top.

5. Transfer Potting Bench Apron and End Patterns on page 20 to front, back, and ends of bench.

Paint the Design:
Clay Pots on Front and Back:
1. Using a #2 flat brush, shade pots with Burnt Sienna mixed with Wicker White.

2. Shade with Light Red Oxide.

3. Re-shade with Burnt Umber.

Clay Pots on Ends:
1. Shade pots with Burnt Sienna mixed with Wicker White.

2. Shade with Light Red Oxide.

3. Re-shade with Burnt Umber.

4. Dry-brush Tapioca highlights in centers.

Greenery:
1. Dip stencil brush in water. Blot on paper towel. Dip one side of brush in Emerald Isle and other side in Fresh Foliage. Pounce greenery in pots, using a light touch to keep it light and airy. Let dry.

Four-petal Flowers:
1. Double-load a #2 flat brush to paint flowers in small and large pots.

2. Paint blue flowers with True Blue and Wicker White, and Yellow Light dotted centers.

3. Paint pink flowers with Magenta and Wicker White, and Yellow Light dotted centers.

4. Paint yellow flowers with Wicker White and Yellow Light, and Emerald Isle dotted centers.

Filler Flowers:
1. Using the handle end of a brush, make dots with Wicker White for flower centers.

Leaves on Large Pots:
1. Using a #2 flat brush, paint leaves with Emerald Isle and Fresh Foliage.

Overall Touches:
1. Dry-brush Burnt Umber on ends, front, and back pieces of bench.

2. Shade areas with Licorice.

3. Using an old toothbrush, spatter top, front, and back of bench with inky Licorice.

Finish:
1. Antique with Down Home Brown. Let dry.

2. Apply waterbase varnish.

Potting Bench Apron Pattern

Enlarge patterns 175%

Potting Bench End Pattern

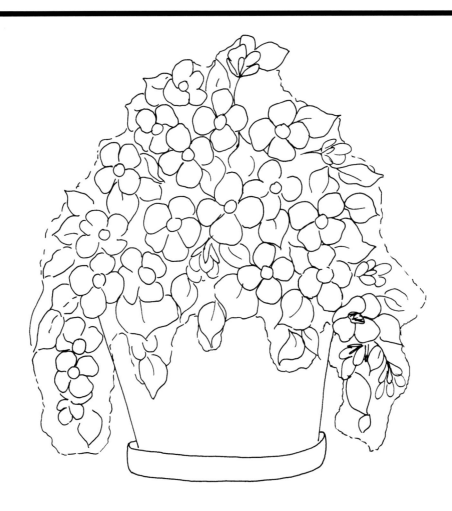

Bunny Plant
Picks & Pot
Instructions begin
on page 22

Bunny Plant Picks & Pot

Pictured on page 21

Designed by
Kirsten Werner

Bunny Patch Picks

GATHER THESE SUPPLIES

Painting Surface:
Plaster of Paris, 1 cup
Plaster molds:
    Bunny & Carrot plant pick
    Bunny & Radish plant pick

Paints, Stains, and Finishes:
Plaster paints:
    Beige
    Black
    Country Blue
    Cream
    Deep Purple
    Ivy
    Terra Cotta
Gloss spray sealer

Brushes:
Round brush, #2
Script liner, #00

INSTRUCTIONS

Prepare:
1. Mold Bunny & Carrot and Bunny & Radish plant picks according to manufacturer's instructions.

Paint the Design:
1. Using a #2 round brush, paint pick colors, using Bunny & Carrot and Bunny & Radish Paint Patterns. Using a #00 script liner, add detail lines with Black. Let dry.

Finish:
1. Apply gloss spray sealer.

Watering Can Pick

GATHER THESE SUPPLIES

Painting Surface:
Plaster of Paris, ½ cup
Plaster mold: Spring Garden

Paints, Stains, and Finishes:
Plaster paints:
    Cream
    Gray
    Ivy
    Terra Cotta
Matte spray sealer

Brushes:
Round brush, #2
Script liner, #00

Bunny & Carrot Paint Pattern

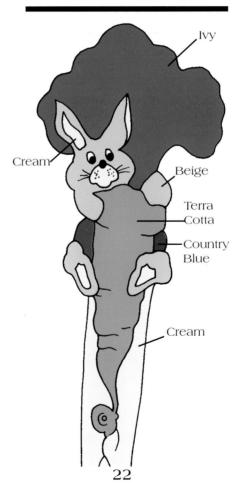

Bunny & Radish Paint Pattern

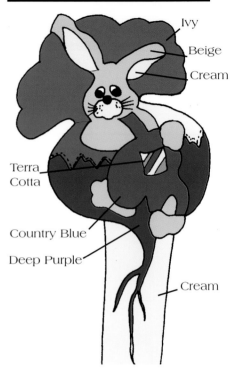

INSTRUCTIONS

Prepare:
1. Mold the watering can pick from the Spring Garden mold, according to manufacturer's instructions.

Paint the Design:
1. Using a #2 round brush, paint watering can with Gray and pick with Cream. Using a #00 script liner, paint stripes and trim with Ivy and spout dots with Terra Cotta. Let dry.

Finish:
1. Apply matte spray sealer.

Plate o' Carrots

GATHER THESE SUPPLIES

Painting Surface:
Wooden plate, 8" dia.

Paints, Stains, and Finishes:
Plaster paints:
  Beige
  Black
  Ivy
  Terra Cotta
Matte spray sealer

Brushes:
Flat brush, #4
Old toothbrush
Round brush, #2

INSTRUCTIONS

Prepare:
1. See Surface Preparation on pages 9-10. Prepare wooden plate.

Paint the Design:
1. Using a #4 flat brush, base-coat plate with Beige. Let dry.

2. Using an old toothbrush, spatter plate with Black.

3. Using a #2 round brush, paint seven carrots with Terra Cotta evenly spaced around rim of plate. Add Ivy carrot foliage. Let dry.

Finish:
1. Apply matte spray sealer.

Purple Pot

GATHER THESE SUPPLIES

Painting Surface:
Clay pot, 6" dia.

Paints, Stains, and Finishes:
Plaster paints:
  Black
  Deep Purple
Matte spray sealer

Brushes:
Old toothbrush
Sponge brush, 1"

INSTRUCTIONS

Prepare:
1. See Surface Preparation on page 9. Prepare clay pot.

Paint the Design:
1. Using a 1" sponge brush, paint rim of pot with Deep Purple.

2. Using an old toothbrush, spatter pot below rim with Black. Let dry.

Finish:
1. Apply matte spray sealer.

Sun, Moon & Stars Pot

Pictured on page 24

Designed by
Sue Bailey

GATHER THESE SUPPLIES

Painting Surface:
Clay pot, 6" dia.
Papîer maché moon on dowel
Papîer maché star on dowel

Paints, Stains, and Finishes:
Acrylic craft paints:
  Burnt Umber
  Yellow Ochre
Metallic acrylic craft paints:
  Blue Sapphire
  Pure Gold
Waterbase varnish

Brushes:
Flat brushes, #2-#10
Scroller, 10/0
Sponge brush, 1"
Stencil brush

Other Supplies:
Acrylic gemstones, blue,
  ¾" dia., (50)

Craft knife
Hot glue gun and glue sticks
Styrofoam ball, 4"
Stencil blank material
Transfer tool
Votive candle, blue
Votive candle holder, blue
  glass

INSTRUCTIONS

Prepare:
1. See Surface Preparation on page 9. Prepare clay pot.

2. Choose a flat brush and base-coat pot with Blue Sapphire.

3. Transfer Sun, Moon & Stars Pot Patterns on page 25 to pot.

4. See Cutting Your Own Stencils on page 87. Transfer Sun, Moon & Stars Pot Patterns on page 25 to stencil blank material. Using a craft knife, cut out stencil.

5. Choose a flat brush and paint papîer maché moon and star with Pure Gold.

Paint the Design:
1. Base-coat moon and sun on pot with Yellow Ochre.

2. See Stenciling Techniques on pages 80-87. Using a stencil brush, stencil stars with Yellow Ochre.

3. Using a 1" sponge brush, paint sun, moon, and stars with two coats of Pure Gold.

4. Using a 10/0 scroller, paint features on sun and moon with Burnt Umber.
Continued on page 25

Sun, Moon & Stars Pot
Instructions begin on page 23

Sun, Moon & Stars Pot Patterns

Patterns are actual size

Continued from page 23

5. Choose a flat brush and float Burnt Umber around nose, on cheeks, and on outer part of pointed rays of sun.

6. Add a wash of Burnt Umber to shade outer curve of moon. Let dry.

Finish:
1. Apply waterbase varnish. Let dry.

2. Using a craft knife, cut a hole in top of styrofoam ball to hold votive candle holder.

3. Paint ball with Blue Sapphire. Let dry. Insert in pot.

4. Place candle holder in styrofoam ball. Hot-glue gemstones around candle holder.

5. Insert moon and star dowels into styrofoam ball. Place candle in candle holder.

Cow Lamp

Pictured on page 26

Designed by
Sue Bailey

GATHER THESE SUPPLIES

Painting Surfaces:
Clay pot, 8" dia.
Clay saucer, 10" dia.

Paints, Stains and Finishes:
Acrylic craft paints:
  Burnt Sienna
  Ivory Black
  Naphthol Crimson
  Portrait Medium
  Titanium White
  Yellow Medium
Gloss sealer spray

Continued on page 27

Cow Lamp
Instructions begin on page 25

Continued from page 25

Brushes:
Flat brushes, #2-#10
Scroller, 10/0

Other Supplies:
Drill and masonry bit
Epoxy
Lamp kit
Lamp shade
Masking tape, 1" wide
Transfer tool

INSTRUCTIONS

Prepare:
1. See Surface Preparation on page 9. Prepare clay pot.

2. Choose a flat brush and base-coat pot with Titanium White. Let dry.

3. Transfer Cow Lamp Pattern below to pot.

4. Base-coat bottom and sides of saucer with Ivory Black. Let dry.

5. Place 1" pieces of masking tape 1" apart across rim, using photo on page 26 as a guide.

6. Paint spaces with Ivory Black. Let dry. Remove tape.

Paint the Design:
Note: Turn pot upside down to paint.

Hearts:
1. Base-coat heart with Naphthol Crimson.

2. Shade with Ivory Black mixed with Naphthol Crimson around cows' heads.

Cows' Bodies:
1. Using a 10/0 scroller, paint spots and outline with Ivory Black. (The white background is the cows' body color.)

2. Choose a flat brush and shade inside ears, on bridge of nose, and between legs to separate with a wash of Ivory Black.

3. Mix Ivory Black with Titanium White. Paint hair on tail and head. Highlight hair on head with Titanium White.

Cows' Eyes:
1. Using a 10/0 scroller, paint eyeball with Titanium White. Paint iris with Burnt Sienna.

2. Paint pupil with Ivory Black. Add a dot of Titanium White to highlight.

3. Outline with Ivory Black above eye. Paint lids with Titanium White.

Cows' Noses and Udders:
1. Choose a flat brush and base-coat noses and udders with Portrait Medium.

2. Shade with Burnt Sienna. Highlight with Titanium White. Detail with Ivory Black.

Cows' Bells:
1. Base-coat bells and rope with Yellow Medium. Shade

Cow Lamp Pattern

Repeat design around pot.

Pattern is actual size

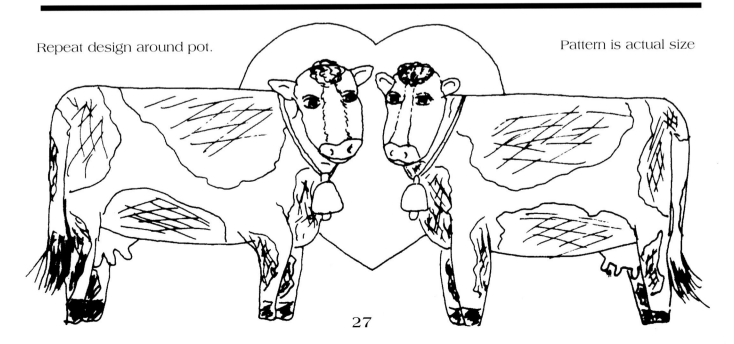

with Burnt Sienna. Highlight with Titanium White mixed with Yellow Medium and Titanium White. Let dry.

Finish:
1. Apply gloss spray sealer.

2. With drill and masonry bit, drill holes for lamp cord in bottom and side of saucer.

3. Install lamp kit, following package instructions. Thread cord through pot and saucer.

4. Turn saucer upside down. Using epoxy, glue pot to saucer. Let dry. Adjust lamp cord.

5. Attach purchased shade or make a shade on a lamp-shade form.

Apples & Daisies Pot

Pictured on page 29

Designed by
Sue Bailey

GATHER THESE SUPPLIES

Painting Surface:
Clay pot, 12" dia.

Paints, Stains, and Finishes:
Acrylic craft paints:
    Alizarin Crimson
    Burnt Umber
    Hunter Green
    Ivory Black
    Raw Sienna
    Red Light
    Titanium White
    Yellow Medium
Waterbase varnish
Continued on page 30

Apples & Daisies Pot Pattern

Enlarge pattern 145%

Repeat design around pot.

Continued from page 28

Brushes:
Angular shader, #8
Flat brushes, #2-#10
Scroller, 10/0

Other Supplies:
Transfer tool

INSTRUCTIONS

Prepare:
1. See Surface Preparation on page 9. Prepare clay pot.

2. Choose a flat brush and base-coat clay pot with Ivory Black. Let dry.

3. Transfer Apples & Daisies Pot Pattern on page 28 to pot.

Paint the Design:
Apples:
1. Base-coat apples with Titanium White. Let dry.

2. Using the Sunflowers, Apples & Daisies Worksheet on page 31, paint apples.

Daisies:
1. Using the Sunflowers, Apples & Daisies Worksheet on page 31, paint daisies.

Leaves and Branches:
1. Base-coat leaves with Hunter Green, allowing Ivory Black background to show. Highlight with Yellow Medium and Titanium White mixed with Yellow Medium. Using a 10/0 scroller, add vein lines with Titanium White mixed with Yellow Medium.

2. Paint branches with Raw Sienna. Shade with Burnt Umber. Highlight with Raw Sienna mixed with Titanium White. Paint squiggles with

Raw Sienna mixed with Titanium White. Let dry.

Finish:
1. Apply waterbase varnish.

Sunflower Pot & Trowel

Pictured on page 32

Designed by
Sue Bailey

GATHER THESE SUPPLIES

Painting Surface:
Clay pot, 10" dia.
Trowel with wooden handle

Paints, Stains, and Finishes:
Acrylic craft paints:
   Burnt Sienna
   Burnt Umber
   Hunter Green
   Ivory Black
   Titanium White
   Yellow Medium
Gloss spray sealer

Brushes:
Deerfoot brush
Flat brushes, #2-#10
Scroller, 10/0

Other Supplies:
All-purpose glue
Artificial sunflower, small
Craft knife
Masking tape, 1" wide
Permanent marker, fine-tip
Plastic liner for pot, 10" dia.
Stencil blank material
Transfer tool

INSTRUCTIONS

Prepare:
1. See Surface Preparation on page 9. Prepare clay pot.

2. See Surface Preparation on pages 9-10. Prepare wooden trowel handle.

3. Choose a flat brush and base-coat pot rim and trowel handle with Ivory Black. Base-coat lower part of pot with Titanium White. Let dry.

4. See Cutting Your Own Stencils on page 87. Transfer Rim Pattern on page 33 to stencil blank material. Using a craft knife, cut stencil.

5. Using a deerfoot brush, paint checks on pot rim with two coats Titanium White. Let dry.

6. Place vertical strips of masking tape 1½" apart to form stripes along bottom part of pot. Paint between strips with Ivory Black. Let dry. Remove tape.

7. Transfer Sunflower Pot & Trowel Pattern on page 33 to pot.

Paint the Design:
1. Using the Sunflowers, Apples & Daisies Worksheet on page 31 paint sunflowers.

2. Place 1" pieces of masking tape 1" apart on trowel handle to create 1" checked design. Paint spaces with Titanium White. Let dry. Remove tape.

Finish:
1. Apply gloss spray sealer to pot and trowel handle.

2. Glue artificial sunflower to handle of trowel.

3. Insert plastic liner into pot.

Sunflowers, Apples & Daisies Worksheet

Sunflowers

1. Choose a flat brush and base-coat petals with Burnt Sienna. Overstroke with Yellow Medium. Paint centers with Burnt Umber. Paint leaves and stems with Hunter Green.

2. Highlight petals with Titanium White mixed with Yellow Medium. Let some Burnt Sienna show through.

3. Using a deerfoot brush, dab flower centers with Burnt Sienna mixed with Yellow Medium.

4. Highlight leaves and stems with Titanium White mixed with Yellow Medium.

5. Using a 10/0 scroller, add vein lines in leaves with Titanium White mixed with Yellow Medium.

Apples

1. Choose a flat brush and base-coat with Titanium White. Let dry.

2. Base-coat with Red Light.

3. Shade with Alizarin Crimson. Add more Red Light, if desired. Blend together. Highlight with Yellow Medium and Titanium White mixed with Yellow Medium. Paint stems with Raw Sienna. Shade with Burnt Umber. Highlight with Raw Sienna and Titanium White.

Daisies

1. Using an angular shader, pick up Titanium White. Starting at outer edge of petal, press chiseled edge of brush down. Pull and lift. Dab Burnt Sienna in center.

2. Highlight petals with Titanium White. Choose a flat brush and dab center with Titanium White mixed with Yellow Medium. Dot center with Ivory Black.

31

Sunflower Pot & Trowel Pattern

Enlarge pattern 300%

Repeat design around pot.

33

Continued on page 35

Repeat design around pot.

Enlarge pattern 300%

Sunshine Farms Box

Pictured on page 34

Designed by
Dianna Marcum

GATHER THESE SUPPLIES

Painting Surface:
Wooden box, 12" x 4¾" x 4"
  with handles

Paints, Stains, and Finishes:
Acrylic craft paints:
  Blue Ribbon
  Buttercrunch
  Dark Gray
  Evergreen
  Forest Green
  French Blue
  Hot Pink
  Licorice
  Primrose
  Tapioca
  Thicket
  Violet Pansy
  Yellow Light
  Yellow Ochre
Antiquing medium:
  Apple Butter Brown
Waterbase varnish

Brushes:
Angular shaders, ¼", ½", ⅜", ⅝"
Deerfoot brush
Flat brush, #4
Liner, #1
Round brush, #3
Sponge brushes, 1", 2"

Sunshine Farms Box
Instructions begin on page 33

Continued from page 33

Other Supplies:
Sandpaper, 220 grit
Tack cloth
Transfer tool

INSTRUCTIONS

Prepare:
1. See Surface Preparation on pages 9-10. Prepare wooden box.

2. Using a 2" sponge brush, base-coat rims and reinforcements with Blue Ribbon. Let dry.

3. Transfer horizon line and sun from Sunshine Farms Box Pattern below to box.

4. Using a 1" sponge brush, base-coat sky area with French Blue.

5. Base-coat sun with Buttercrunch.

6. Base-coat field with Thicket. Let dry.

7. Transfer detail from Sunshine Farms Box Pattern below to front of box.

Paint the Design:
Sky and Sun:
1. Dry-brush a little Tapioca randomly in sky for clouds. Stay toward center of box.

2. Choose an angular shader and float around sun with Yellow Ochre. Dry-brush a little Tapioca in center. Highlight top rounded edge with a float of Yellow Light.

3. Float Yellow Ochre to form sun rays.

4. Shade across bottom of sun with Dark Gray.

5. Using a #1 liner, lightly outline sun with thinned Dark Gray. Add a thin line along one side of each ray.

6. Choose an angular shader and dry-brush cheeks with Primrose. Add Licorice dots for eyes. Add a small highlight on the right side of each eye with Tapioca. Paint eyebrows and nose with Dark Gray.

Large Lettering:
1. Base-coat thick areas with Evergreen.

2. Mix Evergreen with a little Tapioca. Using a dry, #4 flat brush, drag mixture over the letters.

3. Using a #1 liner, lightly outline each letter with thinned Licorice.

Small Lettering:
1. Choose an angular shader and base-coat with Blue Ribbon.

2. Drag a little French Blue over letters to highlight them.

3. Using a #1 liner, outline each letter with thinned Licorice.

Field:
1. Using a deerfoot brush, highlight hilltops with Forest Green.

Flowers:
1. Using a #3 round brush, paint stems and leaves of taller flowers with Thicket

Sunshine Farms Box Pattern

Enlarge pattern 185%

mixed with a touch of Licorice. For blossoms, add small strokes of Violet Pansy.

2. Paint centers of medium size pink flowers with Dark Gray. Float a little Licorice on the left side of each. Paint stems and leaves with Forest Green. Paint petals with Hot Pink mixed with Tapioca.

3. Using a #1 liner, paint asterisks for star-like flowers with Tapioca. Add a dot of Yellow Light in centers. Paint stems and leaves Forest Green. Let dry.

Finish:
1. Sand back box edges for an aged look. Using a tack cloth, wipe away dust.

2. Apply waterbase varnish. Let dry.

3. Antique with Apple Butter Brown. Let dry.

4. Apply an additional coat of waterbase varnish.

Pansies Gift Pot

Pictured on page 37

Designed by
Helen Nicholson

GATHER THESE SUPPLIES

Painting Surfaces:
Clay pot, 10" dia.
Clay saucer, 10" dia.

Paints, Stains, and Finishes:
Acrylic craft paints:
    Bayberry
    Burnt Carmine
    Green Meadow

    Honeycomb
    Licorice
    Maroon
    Nutmeg
    Payne's Gray
    Plum Chiffon
    Raspberry Sherbet
    Rose Pink
    Sunflower
    Taffy
    Wicker White
Waterbase varnish

Brushes:
Angular shader, ⅜"
Round brush, #3
Scroller, 10/0

Other Supplies:
Marine sponge
Transfer tool

INSTRUCTIONS

Prepare:
1. See Surface Preparation on page 9. Prepare clay pot and saucer.

2. Using a #3 round brush, base-coat pot and saucer with Taffy. Let dry.

3. Transfer the Pansies Gift Pot Patterns on page 38 to pot and saucer.

Paint the Design:
Burgundy Pansy Petals:
1. See Pansy Painting Worksheet on page 68. Base-coat the smallest upper petal with Rose Pink.

2. Using a ⅜" angular shader, float with Plum Chiffon.

3. Using a #3 round brush, base-coat mid-petals with Plum Chiffon. Float with Maroon.

4. Base-coat lower petal with Maroon. Shade with Burnt Carmine.

Yellow Pansy Petals:
1. Base-coat petals with Sunflower.

2. Using a ⅜" angular shader, float with Honeycomb.

3. Shade center with Rose Pink.

Burgundy & Yellow Pansy Petals:
1. Using a #3 round brush, base-coat the smallest upper petal with Sunflower.

2. Using a ⅜" angular shader, float with Honeycomb.

3. Using a #3 round brush, base-coat mid-petals with Rose Pink. Float with Raspberry Sherbet.

4. Base-coat lower petal with Raspberry Sherbet. Shade with Maroon.

Pansy Centers:
1. Using a ⅜" angular shader, extend shading around the teardrop centers first with Burnt Carmine and then Licorice.

2. Using a #3 round brush, make teardrop centers with Sunflower. Let dry.

3. Using a ⅜" angular shader, shade left side of teardrops with Nutmeg. Float a highlight of Wicker White on right sides.

4. Using a 10/0 scroller, add fine lines of Licorice to petal centers.

Continued on page 38

Pansies Gift Pot
Instructions begin
on page 36.

Continued from page 36

5. Add fine lines of Wicker White around lower part of teardrops.

6. Using the handle end of a brush, dot right sides of teardrops with Wicker White.

Ribbons and Leaves:
1. Using a #3 round brush, base-coat leaves with Bayberry. Shade with Green Meadow. Let dry. Deepen shading further with a float of Payne's Gray.

2. Base-coat ribbons with Rose Pink. Using a ⅜" angular shader, shade with

Raspberry Sherbet, then with Burnt Carmine. Let dry.

3. Highlight leaves and ribbons with a float of Wicker White. Let dry.

4. Using a 10/0 scroller, add veins to leaves with Payne's Gray.

5. Dot ribbons with Wicker White.

6. Using a ⅜" angular shader, shade around flowers, leaves, and ribbons with a float of Honeycomb. Let dry. Repeat to add depth.

7. Using a #3 round brush,

paint pot rim, and saucer side with Sunflower.

8. Dampen marine sponge with water. Dip in fresh puddle of Wicker White. Squeeze sponge distributing paint. Sponge color around pot rim and saucer sides.

9. Rinse sponge. Repeat sponging with Honeycomb.

10. Using a 10/0 scroller, paint cross-hatch lines with Rose Pink and Wicker White around the pot rim and sides of saucer.

Finish:
1. Apply waterbase varnish.

Pansies Gift Pot Patterns

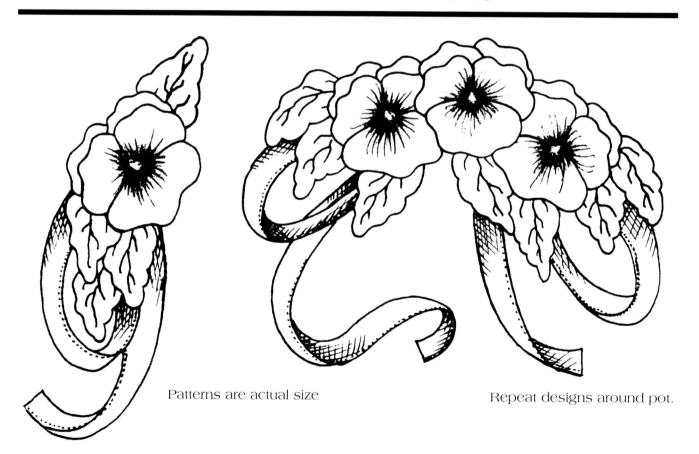

Patterns are actual size

Repeat designs around pot.

Bunny Pot
Instructions begin
on page 40

Bunny Pot

Pictured on page 39

Designed by
Sue Bailey

GATHER THESE SUPPLIES

Painting Surface:
Clay pot, 8" dia.
Wood, ½" thick, 2'

Paints, Stains, and Finishes:
Acrylic craft paints:
    Bayberry
    Burnt Sienna
    Hunter Green
    Ivory Black
    Primrose
    Pure Orange
    Taffy
    Titanium White
    True Blue
    Yellow Medium
Antiquing medium:
    Down Home Brown
Gloss spray sealer
Matte spray sealer

Brushes:
Flat brushes, #2-#10
Scroller, 10/0
Scruffy brush

Other Supplies:
All-purpose glue
Band saw
Floral foam
Paper ribbon, green
Rag
Ruler
Scissors
Spanish moss
Transfer tool

INSTRUCTIONS

Prepare:
1. See Surface Preparation on page 9. Prepare clay pot.

2. Transfer Wooden Carrot Pattern on page 41 to ½" thick wood 12 times.

3. Using a band saw, cut 12 carrots out of wood. See Surface Preparation on page 9. Prepare wood carrots.

Paint the Design:
Carrot Border on Rim:
1. Choose a flat brush and base-coat lower part of pot with Bayberry and rim with Taffy.

2. Base-coat carrots with Pure Orange. Shade with Burnt Sienna. Highlight with Titanium White mixed with Yellow Medium. Using a 10/0 scroller, paint lines with Burnt Sienna.

3. Transfer Bunny Pot Patterns on page 41 to pot.

4. Using a scruffy brush, dab carrot tops with Ivory Black, and Ivory Black mixed with Yellow Medium, and Titanium White mixed with Yellow Medium.

5. Using a 10/0 scroller, paint squiggly lines with Ivory Black.

Bunnies' Fur:
1. Using a scruffy brush, dab on Ivory Black mixed with Titanium White. Then dab again with Titanium White.

2. Using a 10/0 scroller, separate legs, feet, and ears with choppy lines of Ivory Black.

Bunnies' Features:
1. Using a scruffy brush, dab on cheeks, nose, body, and inside ears with Primrose.

2. Choose a flat brush and highlight nose with Titanium White.

3. Paint eyeball with Titanium White. Paint iris with True Blue.

4. Paint pupil with Ivory Black. Add a dot of Titanium White to highlight.

Bows:
1. Base-coat yellow bow with Yellow Medium. Shade with Burnt Sienna. Highlight with Titanium White.

2. Base-coat blue bow with True Blue. Shade with Ivory Black mixed with True Blue. Highlight with Titanium White.

3. Base-coat green bow with Hunter Green. Shade with Hunter Green mixed with Ivory Black. Highlight with Titanium White.

Wooden Carrots:
1. Base-coat with Pure Orange. Let dry.

Finish:
1. Apply matte spray sealer. Let dry.

2. Antique with Down Home Brown, rubbing off most of stain with rag before it dries.

3. Cut 12 pieces of green paper ribbon 7" long to make carrot tops. Cut paper in strips about ½" wide, stopping 2" from bottom end, so strips are still attached. Using scissors, curl each paper strip. Twist paper at bottom, add glue, and push into notch at top of each carrot.

Continued on page 41

Bunny Pot Patterns

Enlarge patterns 120%

Repeat designs around pot.

Wooden Carrot Pattern

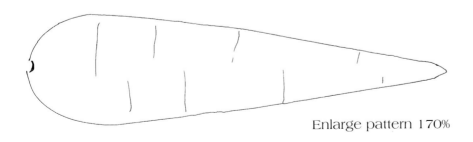

Enlarge pattern 170%

Continued from page 40

4. Apply gloss spray sealer. Let dry.

5. Place floral foam in pot and cover with Spanish moss. Insert wooden carrots.

Elegant Roses Pot

Pictured on page 42

Designed by
Helen Nicholson

GATHER THESE SUPPLIES

Painting Surfaces:
Clay pot, 6" dia.
Clay saucer, 6" dia.

Paints, Stains, and Finishes:
Acrylic gloss enamels:
   Black
   Cranberry Red
   Forest Green
   Holiday Rose
   White
Metallic acrylic craft paint:
   Pure Gold

Brushes:
Flat brush, #8
Round brush, #3
Script liner, #00
Sponge brush, 1"

Other Supplies:
Transfer tool

INSTRUCTIONS

Prepare:
1. See Surface Preparation on page 9. Prepare clay pot and saucer.

Continued on page 43

Elegant Roses Pot
Instructions begin
on page 41

Instructions begin
on page 41

Continued from page 41

2. Using a 1" sponge brush, base-coat saucer and pot with Black.

3. Transfer Elegant Roses Pot Pattern to pot.

4. Paint rims of pot and saucer with Cranberry Red.

Paint the Design:
1. Double-load a #8 flat brush with Cranberry Red and Holiday Rose. Paint an arc for each flower center with the Cranberry Red side of brush toward bottom.

2. Rinse and double-load same brush again with same colors. Add a "U" shaped stroke under center stroke to create flower body.

3. Add two strokes on each side of flower body for petals.

4. Using a #3 round brush, add two comma strokes under each flower with Forest Green.

5. Mix Black with Forest Green; add four strokes between each flower.

6. Mix Forest Green with White. Using a #00 script liner, add fine lines to Black mixed with Forest Green strokes.

7. Add fine lines to each flower center with White. Using the handle end of a brush, add four dots to each flower center with White.

Finish:
1. Paint comma strokes on pot rim and to floral design with Pure Gold.

Elegant Roses Pot Pattern

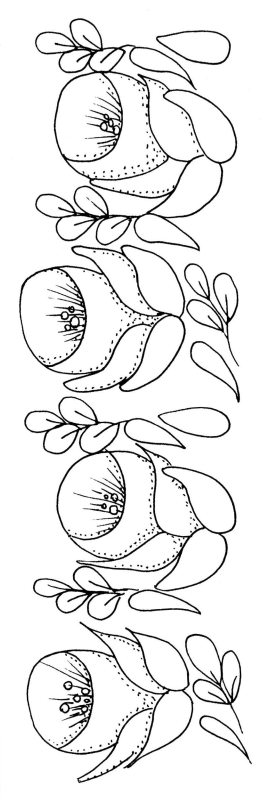

Pattern is actual size

Repeat design around pot.

43

Cherry Pot
Instructions begin on page 45

©1995 Helen Nicholson

Cherry Pot

Pictured on page 44

Designed by
Helen Nicholson

GATHER THESE SUPPLIES

Painting Surfaces:
Clay pot, 7" dia.
Clay saucer, 7" dia.

Paints, Stains, and Finishes:
Acrylic gloss enamels:
   Arbor Green
   Beachcomber Beige
   Coffee Bean
   Cranberry Red
   Dandelion Yellow
   Hot Rod Red
   Mossy Green
   Real Red
   White

Brushes:
Flat brush, #4
Old toothbrush
Round brush, #3
Scroller, 10/0
Sponge brush, 1"

Other Supplies:
Transfer tool

INSTRUCTIONS

Prepare:
1. See Surface Preparation on page 9. Prepare clay pot and saucer.

2. Using a 1" sponge brush, base-coat pot and saucer with White. Let dry.

3. Transfer Cherry Pot Pattern to pot.

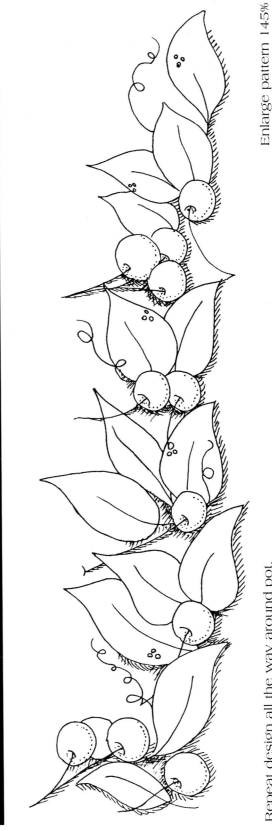

Cherry Pot Pattern

Enlarge pattern 145%

Repeat design all the way around pot.

Paint the Design:
Cherries:
1. Using a #4 flat brush, base-coat cherries with Real Red.

2. Shade left side of each cherry with Hot Rod Red, then Cranberry Red. Shade stem area with Cranberry Red.

3. Highlight each cherry along right side with Dandelion Yellow mixed with White.

Leaves and Stems:
1. Base-coat each leaf with Mossy Green mixed with White.

2. Shade with Mossy Green. Deepen shading further by floating Mossy Green mixed with Arbor Green and White.

3. Using a #3 round brush, detail each leaf with Mossy Green.

4. Using a 10/0 scroller, add tendrils with Arbor Green mixed with inky Mossy Green.

5. Add a stem with Beachcomber Beige. Shade with a bit of Coffee Bean.

6. Using a #4 flat brush, shade outside along left side of each leaf with a coat of Beachcomber Beige.

Finish:
1. Using the handle end of a brush, accent design with White dots. Let dry.

2. Using an old toothbrush, lightly spatter pot and saucer with Coffee Bean, then with Arbor Green.

Wildflower Pot

Pictured on page 48

Designed by
Helen Nicholson

GATHER THESE SUPPLIES

Painting Surfaces:
Clay pot, 7" dia.
Clay saucer, 7" dia.

Paints, Stains, and Finishes:
Acrylic gloss enamels:
   Arbor Green
   Beachcomber Beige
   Bermuda Beach
   Coffee Bean
   Cranberry Red
   Crown Gold
   Dandelion Yellow
   Holiday Rose
   Mossy Green
   Pink Blush
   Real Red
   Rose Wine
   White

Brushes:
Flat brush, #4
Old toothbrush
Round brush, #3
Scroller, 10/0
Sponge brush, 1"

Other Supplies:
Natural sponge
Transfer tool

INSTRUCTIONS

Prepare:
1. See Surface Preparation on page 9. Prepare clay pot and saucer.

2. Using a 1" sponge brush, base-coat saucer and pot with White. Let dry.

3. Transfer Wildflower Pot Pattern on page 47 to pot.

Paint the Design:
Flowers:
1. Using a #3 round brush, base-coat each flower center with Dandelion Yellow.

2. Using a #4 flat brush, shade left side of each flower center with Real Red, then Cranberry Red. Deepen shading further with a float of Coffee Bean.

3. Using a #3 round brush, add petals to each flower center, alternating colors and painting petals from left to right. Use photo on page 48 as a guide. Use the following colors: Cranberry Red, Pink Blush, Dandelion Yellow, Crown Gold, Beachcomber Beige, Bermuda Beach, Holiday Rose, Rose Wine, Real Red.

Stems and Leaves:
Note: Turn pot upside down to paint leaves.

1. Using a 10/0 scroller, add a stem to each flower with Beachcomber Beige.

2. Add leaves with Mossy Green mixed with White. Twist brush while going up pot to vary leaf widths.

3. Add more Mossy Green to mix and add additional leaves all the way around the pot. Add another layer of leaves with Mossy Green.

4. Add Arbor Green to Mossy Green and add another layer of leaves.

5. End with a layer of Arbor Green leaves.

Finish:

1. Using a naural sponge, sponge along bottom edge of pot and upper edge of saucer with Mossy Green mixed with White.

2. Using an old toothbrush, spatter pot and saucer with Beachcomber Beige, Coffee Bean, and White.

Field of Flowers Pattern

Turn flowers sideways and repeat pattern for border on rim.

Enlarge patterns 130%

Wildflower Pot Pattern

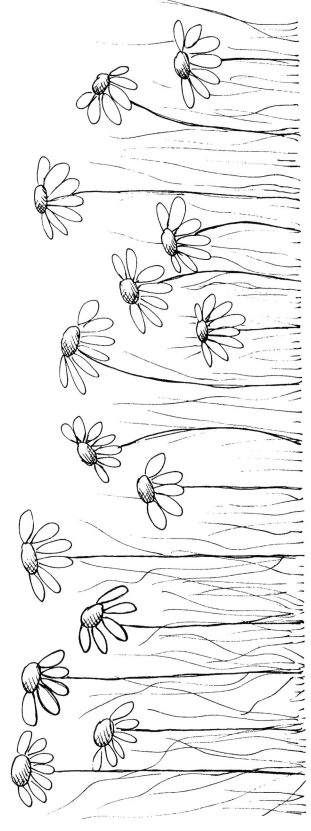

Repeat designs all the way around pots.

Wildflower Pot
Instructions begin
on page 46

Field of
Flowers Pot
Instructions begin
on page 50

Crocus Pot
Instructions begin
on page 50

Field of Flowers Pot

Pictured on page 49

Designed by
Helen Nicholson

GATHER THESE SUPPLIES

Painting Surfaces:
Clay pot, 6" dia.
Clay saucer, 6" dia.

Paints, Stains, and Finishes:
Acrylic gloss enamels:
   Cranberry Red
   Mossy Green
   Pink Blush
   Rose Wine
   White

Brushes:
Round brush, #3
Scroller, 10/0
Sponge brush, 1"

Other Supplies:
Natural sponge
Satin picot ribbon, green,
   ⅜" wide, 6" long
Transfer tool

INSTRUCTIONS

Prepare:
1. See Surface Preparation on page 9. Prepare clay pot and saucer.

2. Using a 1" sponge brush, base-coat pot and saucer with White. Let dry.

3. Transfer Field of Flowers Pattern on page 47 onto pot. Place flowers on stems around bottom of pot.

4. Using a natural sponge, sponge lower 1¼" of pot with Mossy Green mixed with White. Let dry.

Paint the Design:
1. Using a #3 round brush, paint flower petals with Pink Blush.

2. For flower centers, alternate White and Cranberry Red dots.

3. Using a 10/0 scroller, add stems and leaves to each flower with Mossy Green mixed with White.

4. Add a heart between each flower/leaf group in borders with Rose Wine.

Finish:
1. Loop green satin picot ribbon around pot under rim. Tie ends in a bow.

Crocus Pot

Pictured on page 49

Designed by
Helen Nicholson

GATHER THESE SUPPLIES

Painting Surfaces:
Clay pot, 5" dia.
Clay saucer, 5" dia.

Paints, Stains, and Finishes:
Acrylic gloss enamels:
   Arbor Green
   Beachcomber Beige
   Crown Gold
   Lavender
   Mossy Green
   Purple Velvet
   Real Yellow
   White

Brushes:
Flat brush, #4
Liner, #1
Old toothbrush
Round brush, #3
Sponge brush, 1"

Other Supplies:
Natural sponge
Transfer tool

INSTRUCTIONS

Prepare:
1. See Surface Preparation on page 9. Prepare clay pot and saucer.

2. Using a 1" sponge brush, base-coat saucer and pot with White. Let dry.

3. Transfer Crocus Pot Top Edge and Bottom Patterns on page 51 to pot.

Paint the Design:
First Flower:
1. Using a #3 round brush, base-coat with Real Yellow mixed with White.

2. Using a #4 flat brush, shade outer petals with Crown Gold. Highlight center petal along upper right with White. Work quickly and blend colors while wet.

Second Flower:
1. Using a #3 round brush, base-coat with Lavender.

2. Using a #4 flat brush, shade outer petals with Lavender and a small amount of Purple Velvet. Also shade bottom of center petal with same mix. Highlight center petal along upper right with White.

Third Flower:

1. Using a #3 round brush, base-coat with Real Yellow mixed with White.

2. Using a #4 flat brush, shade outer petals with Crown Gold. Highlight center petal along upper right with White.

Fourth Flower:

1. Using a #3 round brush, base-coat with Purple Velvet mixed with Lavender.

2. Using a #4 flat brush, shade outer petals and bottom of center petal with Purple Velvet. Highlight center petal along upper right with White.

Fifth Flower:

1. Using a #3 round brush, base-coat with White mixed with a bit of Real Yellow.

2. Using a #4 flat brush, shade outer petals with Crown Gold. Highlight center petal along upper right with White.

Sixth Flower:

1. Using a #3 round brush, base-coat with White mixed with Lavender.

2. Using a #4 flat brush, shade outer petals and center petal with Lavender. Deepen shading while wet by adding a bit of Purple Velvet to the mix. Highlight center petal along upper right with White.

Seventh Flower:

1. Using a #3 round brush, base-coat with Lavender.

Continued on page 52

Crocus Pot Top Edge Pattern

Crocus Pot Bottom Pattern

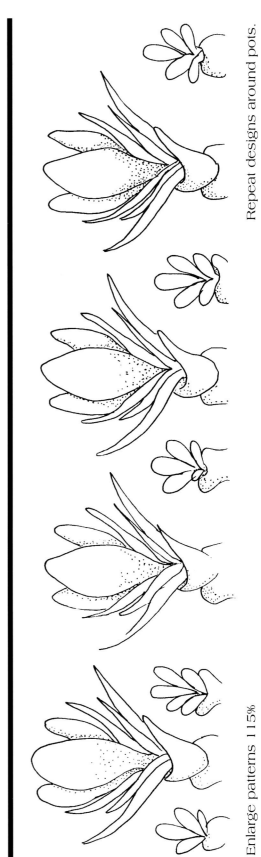

Repeat designs around pots.

Enlarge patterns 115%

Continued from page 51

2. Using a #4 flat brush, shade outer petals with Purple Velvet. Highlight center petal along upper right with White.

Leaves:
Note: Turn pot upside down to paint leaves.

1. Using a #3 round brush, add leaves on each side of flower with a mix of Arbor Green and Mossy Green.

2. Add leaves over the previous leaves with Mossy Green. All leaves overlap at base of flower.

3. Turn pot right side up. Using a #1 liner, paint leaf stems with Beachcomber Beige mixed with Mossy Green.

4. Add Mossy Green strokes between each flower with Mossy Green. Blend Beachcomber Beige, Mossy Green, and White in equal portions and add final stroke to bottom of each flower with mix.

Pot Bottom:
1. Using a natural sponge, sponge bottom of pot with Lavender mixed with White.

2. Add stroke leaves to edge of pot with Lavender.

3. Using the handle end of a brush, add dots of Purple Velvet.

Finish:
1. Using an old toothbrush, spatter with Purple Velvet.

Chicken 'n Biscuits Pot

Pictured on page 53

Designed by
Helen Nicholson

GATHER THESE SUPPLIES

Painting Surfaces:
Clay pot, 7" dia.
Clay saucer, 7" dia.

Paints, Stains, and Finishes:
Acrylic gloss enamels:
  Black
  Coffee Bean
  Dandelion Yellow
  Dolphin Gray
  Hot Rod Red
  Tangerine
  White

Brushes:
Flat brush, #4
Liner, #1
Old toothbrush
Round brush, #3
Sponge brush, 1"

Other Supplies:
Compressed sponge
Craft knife
Permanent marker, fine-tip
  black
Ruler
Transfer tool

INSTRUCTIONS

Prepare:
1. See Surface Preparation on page 9. Prepare clay pot and saucer.

2. Using a 1" sponge brush, base-coat pot with Black.

3. Base-coat saucer with Hot Rod Red. Let dry.

4. Transfer Chicken 'n Biscuits Pot Pattern on page 54 to pot.

Paint the Design:
1. Base-coat chickens with White.

2. Using a #3 round brush, base-coat combs with Hot Rod Red. Highlight with a float of Tangerine.

3. Base-coat feet and beaks with Dandelion Yellow. Shade with Tangerine.

4. Using a #1 liner, paint inside mouths with thinned Coffee Bean.

5. Paint tongues and hearts with Hot Rod Red.

6. Using a #4 flat brush, shade with a double-loaded brush of Dolphin Gray and White.

7. Paint Black comma strokes for eyes. Shade with White; add a White highlight dot to each. Let dry.

Finish:
1. Add details with black permanent marker.

2. Measure height of rim. Divide measurement by 3. Using a craft knife, cut a square from sponge, using final measurements.
Continued on page 54

Chicken 'n Biscuits Pot
Instructions begin on page 52

Small Crow Pot
Instructions begin on page 54

Continued from page 52

3. Moisten sponge. Squeeze out excess water. Dip sponge into Hot Rod Red. Sponge a three row checkerboard around rim of pot.

4. Using a #1 liner, add White lines along edges of checks.

5. Using an old toothbrush, spatter pot and saucer with White.

Chicken 'n Biscuits Pot Pattern

Pattern is actual size

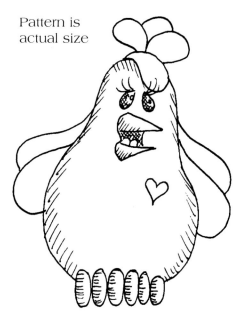

Repeat design around pot.

Small Crow Pot

Pictured on page 53

Designed by
Helen Nicholson

GATHER THESE SUPPLIES

Painting Surface:
Clay pot, 2½" dia.

Paints, Stains, and Finishes:
Acrylic gloss enamels:
  Beachcomber Beige
  Black
  Dandelion Yellow
  Hot Rod Red
  Real Green
  Tangerine
  White

Brushes:
Liner, #1
Sponge brush, 1"

Other Supplies:
Masking tape
Measuring tape
Natural sponge
Pencil
Scissors
Sponge brush, 1"
Stencil: Backyard Birdhouse
Transfer tool

INSTRUCTIONS

Prepare:
1. See Surface Preparation on page 9. Prepare clay pot.

2. Using a 1" sponge brush, base-coat pot with Beach-comber Beige. Let dry.

Stencil:
Note: Use only the crow design from the Backyard Birdhouse stencil; masking out surrounding designs with tape.

1. Using a measuring tape, measure circumference of pot and divide by three. Mark placement for three crows.

2. Using masking tape, secure stencil on pot at first marking.

3. Moisten sponge. Squeeze out excess water. Sponge crow with Black. Remove stencil. Reposition stencil two more times and sponge.

Paint the Design:
Crows:
1. Using a #1 liner, paint crows' beaks and legs with Tangerine.

2. Dot an eye on each with White.

Flowers, Leaves:
1. See Simple Brush Strokes on page 13. Using the handle end of a brush, paint a dot heart with Hot Rod Red between crows. Using a #1 liner, paint stem and leaves with Real Green.

Grass:
Note: Turn pot upside down to paint grass.

1. Paint blades with Real Green, then highlight with Dandelion Yellow.

Finish:
1. Cut a small square of sponge from a 1" sponge brush. Use sponge square to stamp two rows of checks with Beachcomber Beige around rim of pot. See photo on page 53 as guide.

2. Using a #1 liner, add fine White lines along edges of checks.

Daisies & Checks Pots

Pictured on page 55

Designed by
Helen Nicholson

GATHER THESE SUPPLIES

Painting Surfaces:
Clay pot, 6" dia.
Clay pot, 2⅓" dia.
Clay saucer, 6" dia.

Paints, Stains, and Finishes:
Acrylic gloss enamels:
   Black
   Cranberry Red
   Dandelion Yellow
   Dolphin Gray
   Mossy Green
   Real Red
   White

Brushes:
Deerfoot brush
Flat brush, #4
Liner, #1
Old toothbrush
Round brush, #3
Sponge brush, 1"

Other Supplies:
Masking tape
Paper towel
Stencil: Checkerboard Border
Transfer tool

INSTRUCTIONS

Prepare:
1. See Surface Preparation on page 9. Prepare clay pots and saucer.

2. Using a 1" sponge brush, base-coat saucer and pots with Dolphin Gray. Let dry.

3. Transfer Daisies & Checks Small Pot and Large Pot Patterns to pots.

Paint the Design:
1. Using a #3 round brush, base-coat each flower center with Real Red.

2. Using a #4 flat brush, float left side of each flower center with Cranberry Red. Using a deerfoot brush, tap left side of shade with Cranberry Red.

3. Stipple along right side of each flower center with Dandelion Yellow.

4. Using a #1 liner, paint a fine line under each flower center of Mossy Green.

5. Using a #3 round brush, stroke leaves along each side of flower stem with Mossy Green.

6. Stroke petals around each flower center with White.

7. Using a #1 liner, add fine cross-hatching to right side of each flower center with White.

8. Load a deerfoot brush with Mossy Green. Wipe most of paint from brush with a paper towel. Add grass along bottom edge of saucer and pot. To create wispy blades, hold pot upside down and pull brush from bottom approximately ¾". Hold brush gently and allow bristles to barely touch pot.

Daisies & Checks Small Pot Pattern

Daisies & Checks Large Pot Pattern

Repeat designs around pots.   Enlarge patterns 250%

Finish:
1. Using masking tape, secure the Checkerboard Border stencil to the large pot rim. Stencil with Black.

2. Using a #4 flat brush, paint a checkerboard on small pot with Black.

3. Using a #1 liner, highlight both pots with fine lines of White. Let dry.

4. Using an old toothbrush, spatter pots with White.

Rose Clay Pots

Pictured on page 58

Designed by
Donna Dewberry

GATHER THESE SUPPLIES

Painting Surface:
Clay pot, 6" dia.
Clay pot, 5" dia.
Clay pot, 4" dia.

Paints, Stains, and Finishes:
Acrylic craft paints:
    Berry Wine
    Green Forest
    Wicker White
Spray paint:
    Black
Matte spray sealer

Brushes:
Flat brushes, #12, ¾"
Script liner, #2

Other Supplies:
Transfer tool

INSTRUCTIONS

Prepare:
1. See Surface Preparation on page 9. Prepare clay pots.

2. Spray pots inside and out with Black. Let dry.

3. Transfer Rose Clay Pots Patterns to side of pots.

Paint the Design:
1. See Rosebuds & Roses Worksheet on page 62. Using a #12 flat brush, paint rosebuds and roses with Berry Wine and Wicker White.

2. Paint leaves with Green Forest and Wicker White.

3. Using a #2 script liner, paint curlicues with inky Green Forest.

Finish:
1. Apply matte spray sealer.

Rose Clay Pots Patterns

4" Pot

5" Pot

6" Pot

Repeat designs around pots.

Enlarge patterns 215%

Rose Watering Can
Instructions begin
on page 59

Rose Clay Pots
Instructions begin
on page 57

Rose Watering Can

Pictured on page 58

Designed by
Donna Dewberry

GATHER THESE SUPPLIES

Painting Surface:
Oval tin watering can,
  8" x 5" x 7"

Paints, Stains, and Finishes:
Acrylic craft paints:
  Berry Wine
  Green Forest
  Wicker White
Spray paint:
  Black
Matte spray sealer

Brushes:
Flat brushes, #12, ¾"
Script liner, #2

Other Supplies:
Transfer tool

INSTRUCTIONS

Prepare:
1. See Surface Preparation on page 10. Prepare tin watering can.

2. Spray watering can with Black spray paint. Let dry.

3. Transfer Rose Watering Can Top Pattern to top of watering can.

4. Transfer Rose Watering Can Side Pattern to side of watering can.

Paint the Design:
1. See Rosebuds & Roses Worksheet on page 62. Using a #12 flat brush, paint rosebuds and roses with Berry Wine and Wicker White.

2. Paint leaves with Green Forest and Wicker White.

3. Using a #2 script liner, paint curlicues with inky Green Forest.

4. Paint criss-cross design on end of spout with Green Forest. Let dry.

Finish:
1. Apply matte spray sealer.

Rose Watering Can Top Pattern

Rose Watering Can Side Pattern

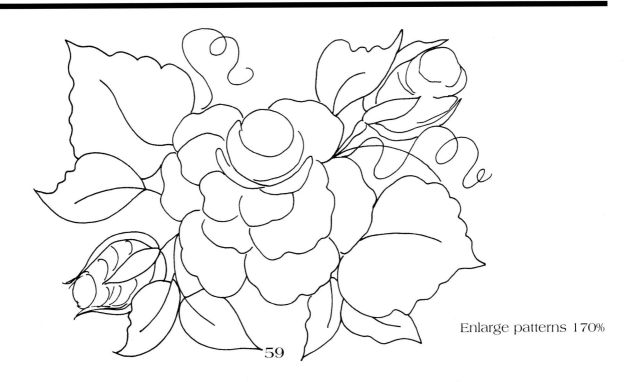

Enlarge patterns 170%

Roses Pots & Pot Stand

Pictured on page 61

Designed by
Donna Dewberry

GATHER THESE SUPPLIES

Painting Surfaces:
Clay pots, 3½" dia. (3)
Wooden pot stand,
    14¼" x 4¼" x 4"

Paints, Stains, and Finishes:
Acrylic craft paints:
    Country Twill
    Green Forest
    Night Blue
    Rose Chiffon
    Wicker White
Matte spray sealer

Brushes:
Flat brushes, #12, ¾"
Script liner, #2

Other Supplies:
Transfer tool

INSTRUCTIONS

Prepare:
1. See Surface Preparation on pages 9-10. Prepare clay pots and wooden pot stand.

2. Using a #12 flat brush, base-coat pots and stand with Wicker White.

3. Transfer Roses Pots Pattern to pots.

4. Transfer Roses Pot Stand Pattern to stand.

Paint the Design:
1. See One Stroke Painting Worksheet on page 63. Paint vines of wreath with Country Twill and Wicker White.

2. See Rosebuds & Roses Worksheet on page 62. Paint rosebuds and roses with Rose Chiffon and Wicker White.

3. Using a #2 script liner, paint ribbons with Night Blue and Wicker White.

4. Using a ¾" flat brush, paint leaves with Green Forest and Wicker White.

5. Paint curlicues with inky Green Forest.

Finish:
1. Apply matte spray sealer.

Roses Pots Pattern

Roses Pot Stand Pattern

Enlarge patterns 180%

Rosebuds & Roses Worksheet

Rosebuds

Double-load a #12 flat brush with Berry Wine or Rose Chiffon and Wicker White.

Push "up the hill" back to chisel edge, and lift with Wicker White always turned upward.

Fill in additional strokes.

Chisel edge.

Make second stroke with Wicker White upward, going "down the hill" to make a "U".

Make 5 or 6 petals, overlapping to form a circle.

Roses

Overlap petals.

Push, wiggle slightly, and lift to chisel edge.

Add next layer of petals to form next "skirt".

Chisel edge filler petals around bud.

Vines

Double-load Dark Brown and Wicker White.

Completed Rose

Chisel Edge Leaves

Push.

Turn.

Lift to chisel edge.

Leaves

Double-load a ¾" flat brush with Green Forest and Wicker White.

Wiggle, turn, and lift.

Stem

62

One Stroke Painting Worksheet

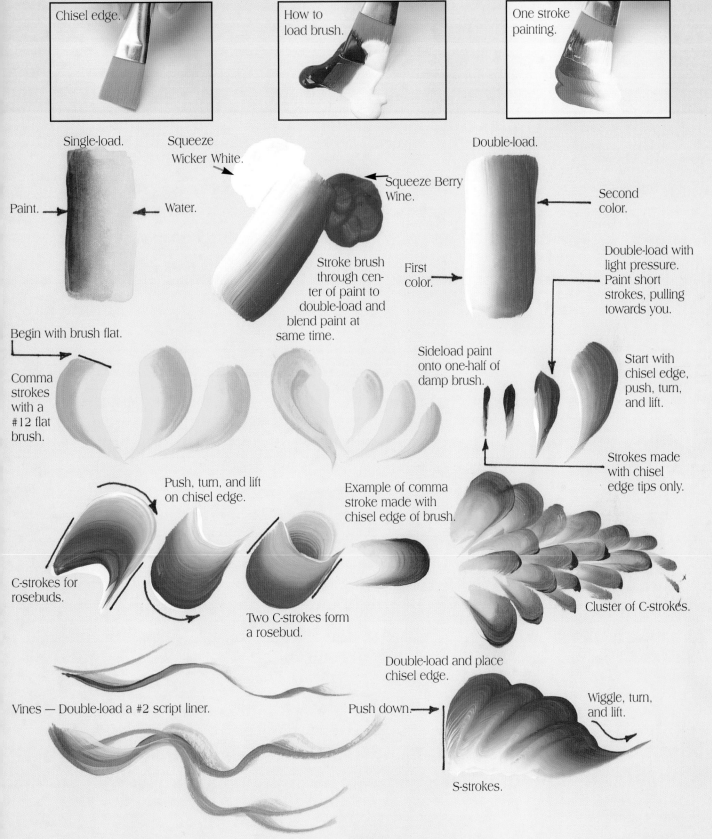

Chisel edge.

How to load brush.

One stroke painting.

Single-load.

Squeeze Wicker White.

Double-load.

Paint.

Water.

Squeeze Berry Wine.

Stroke brush through center of paint to double-load and blend paint at same time.

Second color.

First color.

Double-load with light pressure. Paint short strokes, pulling towards you.

Begin with brush flat.

Comma strokes with a #12 flat brush.

Sideload paint onto one-half of damp brush.

Start with chisel edge, push, turn, and lift.

Strokes made with chisel edge tips only.

Push, turn, and lift on chisel edge.

Example of comma stroke made with chisel edge of brush.

C-strokes for rosebuds.

Two C-strokes form a rosebud.

Cluster of C-strokes.

Vines — Double-load a #2 script liner.

Double-load and place chisel edge.

Push down.

Wiggle, turn, and lift.

S-strokes.

63

Iris Box
Instructions begin
on page 65

Pansy Basket
Instructions begin
on page 65

Iris Box

Pictured on page 64

Designed by
Donna Dewberry

GATHER THESE SUPPLIES

Painting Surface:
Papîer maché box with lid,
   14" x 6" x 6"

Paints, Stains, and Finishes:
Acrylic craft paints:
   Antique Gold
   Dioxazine Purple
   Green Forest
   School Bus Yellow
   Wicker White
Spray paint:
   White
Matte spray sealer

Brushes:
Flat brush, #12
Script liner, #2
Scruffy brush

Other Supplies:
Transfer tool

INSTRUCTIONS

Prepare:
1. See Surface Preparation on page 10. Prepare papîer maché box.

2. Spray box with White. Let dry.

3. Using a scruffy brush, pounce brush around edge of box lid with Dioxazine Purple and Wicker White. Let dry.

4. Transfer Iris Box Pattern on page 66 to sides of box, transferring one flower to each side of the box.

Paint the Design:
1. See Iris Worksheet on page 67. Using a #12 flat brush, paint petals with Dioxazine Purple and Wicker White.

2. Paint leaves with Green Forest and Wicker White.

3. Using a #2 script liner, paint curlicues with inky Green Forest.

Finish:
1. Apply matte spray sealer.

Pansy Basket

Pictured on page 64

Designed by
Donna Dewberry

GATHER THESE SUPPLIES

Painting Surface:
Tin basket, 8½" x 5½"

Paints, Stains, and Finishes:
Acrylic craft paints:
   Dioxazine Purple
   Green Forest
   School Bus Yellow
   Wicker White
Spray paint:
   White
Matte spray sealer

Brushes:
Flat brush, #12
Script liner, #2

Other Supplies:
Transfer tool

INSTRUCTIONS

Prepare:
1. See Surface Preparation on page 10. Prepare tin basket.

2. Spray basket with White. Let dry.

3. Using a #12 flat brush, paint handle Green Forest. Let dry.

4. Transfer Pansy Basket Pattern on page 69 to front of basket.

Paint the Design:
1. See Pansies Worksheet on page 68. Paint upper three petals of three pansies with Dioxazine Purple and Wicker White.

2. Paint upper three petals in remaining pansy with School Bus Yellow and Wicker White.

3. Paint lower petals with Dioxazine Purple and School Bus Yellow.

4. Paint pansy centers with Green Forest and School Bus Yellow.

5. Paint leaves with Green Forest and School Bus Yellow. Let dry.

6. Using a #2 script liner, paint stems with inky Green Forest.

Finish:
1. Apply matte spray sealer.

Iris Box Pattern

Enlarge pattern 120%

Iris Worksheet

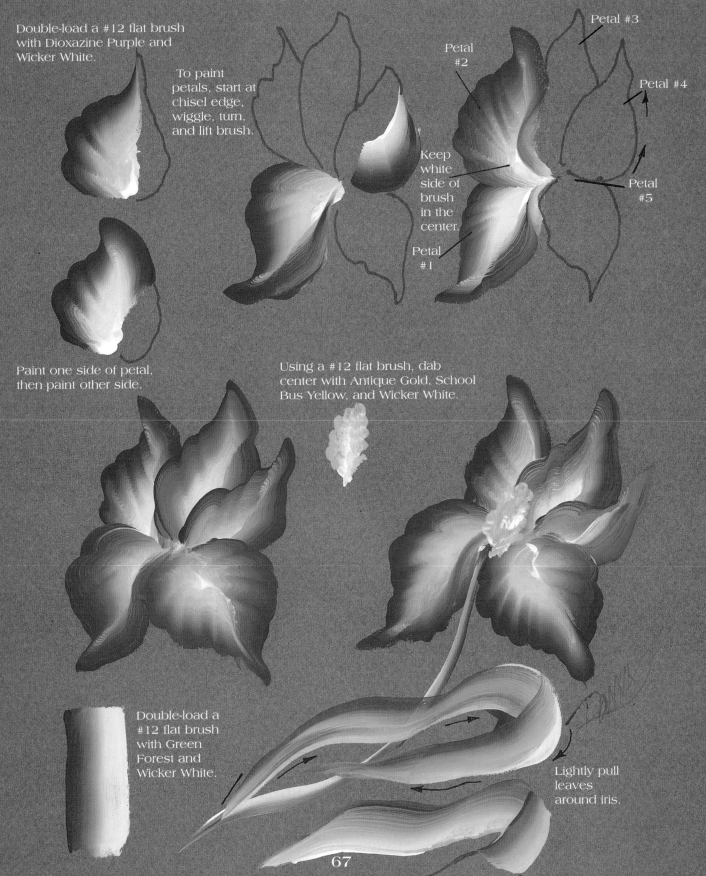

Double-load a #12 flat brush with Dioxazine Purple and Wicker White.

To paint petals, start at chisel edge, wiggle, turn, and lift brush.

Keep white side of brush in the center.

Petal #2

Petal #3

Petal #4

Petal #5

Petal #1

Paint one side of petal, then paint other side.

Using a #12 flat brush, dab center with Antique Gold, School Bus Yellow, and Wicker White.

Double-load a #12 flat brush with Green Forest and Wicker White.

Lightly pull leaves around iris.

Pansies Worksheet

Double-load a #12 flat brush with Dioxazine Purple and Wicker White.

For lower petals, double-load with Dioxazine Purple and School Bus Yellow.

For leaves, double-load with Green Forest and School Bus Yellow.

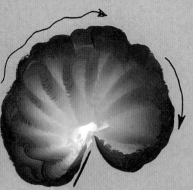

To form petals, start on chisel edge and wiggle brush in a circle.

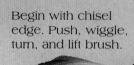

Double-load with Green Forest and School Bus Yellow. Lightly push chisel edge against surface in pansy center.

Begin with chisel edge. Push, wiggle, turn, and lift brush.

Paint one side of leaf, then paint the other side. Pull stem through leaf with chisel edge of brush.

Paint top three petals first.

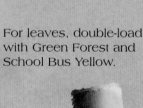

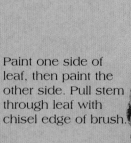

For yellow pansies, double-load with School Bus Yellow and Wicker White.

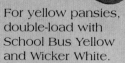

68

Pattern is actual size

Apples Flower Pot

Pictured on page 70

Designed by
Chris Stokes

GATHER THESE SUPPLIES

Painting Surfaces:
Clay pot, 7" dia.
Dowels, ¼" dia., 8" long (3)
Wood, 2', ½" thick

Paints, Stains, and Finishes:
Acrylic craft paints:
   Alizarian Crimson
   Burnt Carmine
   Christmas Red
   Clover
   English Mustard
   Licorice
   Red Light
   Southern Pine
   Sunflower
   Tapioca
Antiquing medium:
   Down Home Brown
Waterbase varnish

Brushes:
Deerfoot brush
Flat brushes, #6, ½"
Liner, #2
Old toothbrush
Round brush, #3

Other Supplies:
Artificial greenery
Band saw
Drill and ¼" drill bit
Floral foam
Spanish moss
Transfer tool
Wood glue

INSTRUCTIONS

Prepare:
1. See Surface Preparation on page 9. Prepare clay pot.

2. Using a ½" flat brush, base-coat bottom part of pot with Sunflower and rim with Alizarian Crimson. Let dry.

3. Transfer Apples Flower Pot Pattern on page 71 to pot.

Apple Picks:
1. Transfer Apple Pick Pattern on page 71 three times to ½" wood.

2. Using band saw, cut out apples. See Surface Preparation on page 10. Prepare wood apples.

3. Drill a hole in bottom of each apple. Dip one end of each dowel in wood glue and insert in each apple. Let dry.

4. Stain apple picks with Down Home Brown.
Continued on page 71

Apples Flower Pot

Instructions begin
on page 69

Continued from page 69

Paint the Design:
Apple on Pot:
1. See Sunflowers, Apples & Daisies Worksheet on page 31, paint apples.

2. Float Christmas Red shading on both sides of apple. Let dry.

3. Repeat shading on right side of apple. Repeat on right side with Alizarian Crimson to build depth. Repeat for more depth with Burnt Carmine.

4. Highlight with dry-brushed Tapioca.

Branch:
1. Using a #3 round brush, paint branch with English Mustard and Licorice.

2. Highlight with Tapioca.

Leaves:
1. Paint a few leaves with double-loaded Southern Pine and Sunflower.

2. Paint other leaves with double-loaded Clover and Sunflower.

Blossoms:
1. Using a #6 flat brush, double-load Alizarian Crimson and Tapioca. Paint petals.

2. Using a deerfoot brush, stipple centers with Clover and Sunflower.

3. Using a #2 liner, paint tendrils with an inky consistency of one of the green leaf mixes.

Lettering on Rim of Pot:
1. Using a #3 round brush, paint lettering with Tapioca. Let dry.

Apple Picks:
1. Using a #2 liner, paint stems with inky Clover.

2. Using a #3 round brush, paint fronts with Sunflower.

3. See Sunflowers, Apples & Daisies Worksheet on page 31, shade and highlight red apples. Shade and highlight green apple with Clover and Southern Pine.

4. Paint a few leaves with double-loaded Southern Pine and Sunflower.

5. Paint other leaves with double-loaded Clover and Sunflower.

Finish:
1. Dilute Down Home Brown with water. Antique pot. Let dry.

2. Using an old toothbrush, spatter pot, with diluted Down Home Brown.

3. Apply waterbase varnish to inside and outside of pot and to apple picks.

4. Put floral foam in pot. Cover with Spanish moss. Insert stems of artificial greenery in floral foam. Insert apple picks among greenery.

Apples Flower Pot Pattern

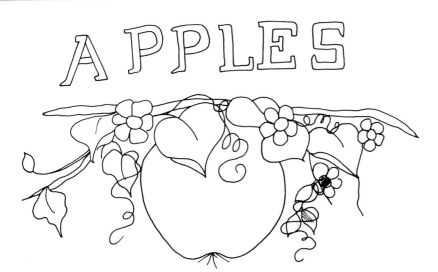

Apple Pick Pattern

Enlarge patterns 130%

Clay Pot Bird Bath
Instructions begin on page 73

Clay Pot Bird Bath

Pictured on page 72

Designed by
Chris Stokes

GATHER THESE SUPPLIES

Painting Surfaces:
Clay pot, 4" dia.
Clay saucer, 4" dia.

Paints, Stains, and Finishes:
Acrylic craft paints:
　Burnt Umber
　Coastal Blue
　Cobalt Blue
　Dioxazine Purple
　Fresh Foliage
　Lavender
　Molasses
　Old Ivy
　Raspberry Wine
　Rose Crimson
　Sunflower
　Taffy
　Titanium White
　Yellow Ochre
Waterbase varnish

Brushes:
Angular shader, ¼"
Flat brush, #10
Liner, #2
Stencil brush
Sponge brush, 2"

Other Supplies:
Birds, 2" to 3" long
Dried flowers and berries
Green moss
Hot glue gun and glue sticks
Transfer tool

Prepare:
1. See Surface Preparation on page 9. Prepare clay pot and saucer.

2. Turn pot upside down. Hot-glue saucer right side up to bottom (now top) of pot.

3. Using a 2" sponge brush, base-coat about half the height of the clay pot with Coastal Blue. Start at bottom and work upward.

4. Touch corner of sponge brush in Cobalt Blue and work darker color to top of saucer.

5. Using a stencil brush, make a circular motion to form clouds with Taffy. Let dry.

6. Transfer Clay Pot Bird Bath Pattern on page 74 to pot.

Paint the Design:
House:
1. Using a ¼" angular shader, float roof with Raspberry Wine.

2. Float walls with Taffy.

3. Shade windows with Burnt Umber.

4. Paint door with Raspberry Wine.

Path:
1. Using a #10 flat brush, base-coat path with Sunflower.

2. Highlight with Taffy.

3. Shade with Molasses.

Hilly Yard:
1. Paint ground with Old Ivy.

2. Highlight some hills with Fresh Foliage.

Trees, Shrubs, and Flowers:
1. Using a ¼" angular shader, pounce trees in background with Old Ivy and a touch of Taffy.

2. Using a stencil brush, pounce wisteria with Dioxazine Purple mixed with Taffy.

3. Leave wisteria color in the brush and pick up Rose Crimson and mix with Titanium White. Pounce in redbud trees.

4. Using a ¼" angular shader, pounce some flowers with Lavender mixed with Rose Crimson and Titanium White.

5. Paint yellow flowers with double-loaded Yellow Ochre mixed with Titanium White and Cobalt Blue mixed with Taffy.

Fence:
1. Using a #2 liner, stroke fence with Taffy then Titanium White.

Flowers Around Fence:
1. Using a ¼" angular shader, pounce in with double-loaded Titanium White mixed with Yellow Ochre and Cobalt Blue mixed with Taffy. Let dry.

Finish:
1. Using a 2" sponge brush, apply waterbase varnish. Let dry.

2. Hot-glue green moss around edges of bird bath (saucer).

3. Hot-glue dried flowers and berries on the green moss. Hot-glue birds on bird bath.

Clay Pot Bird Bath Pattern

Extend fence, yard, bushes, and flowers around pot.

Pattern is actual size

Herb Pot

Pictured on page 75

Designed by
Peggy Caldwell

GATHER THESE SUPPLIES

Painting Surfaces:
Papîer maché flower pot,
  5" dia., with green/brown
  gingham design
Rusty tin round plant pick

Paints, Stains, and Finishes:
Acrylic craft paints:
  Basil Green
  Icy White
Matte spray sealer

Brushes:
Flat brush, ¾"
Script liner, #00

Other Supplies:
Permanent marker, brown
Ruler

INSTRUCTIONS

Prepare:
1. See Surface Preparation on page 10. Prepare papîer maché pot and tin plant pick.

Paint the Design:
1. Using a ¾" flat brush, paint a 1⅛" wide band around pot below rim with Basil Green. Let dry.

2. Using a brown permanent marker, write herb names on band in ¾" high letters.

Finish:
1. Apply matte spray sealer to pot and plant pick. Let dry.

2. Using a #00 script liner, write "HERBS" on plant pick with Icy White.

Potted Herb Heart Boxes

Pictured on page 75

Designed by
Peggy Caldwell

GATHER THESE SUPPLIES

Painting Surfaces:
Nested papîer maché heart-shaped boxes with green/ brown gingham design (3)

Paints, Stains, and Finishes:
Acrylic craft paints:
  Basil Green
  Burnt Umber
  Fresh Foliage
  Icy White
  Leaf Green
  Maple Syrup
  Red Violet

Continued on page 76

Herb Pot
Instructions begin
on page 74

Potted Herb
Heart Boxes
Instructions begin
on page 74

Potted Herb Photo Frame
Instructions begin on page 76

Continued from page 74

Strawberry Parfait
Wintergreen
Matte spray sealer
Painting medium:
  extender

Brushes:
Flat brushes, #12, ¾"
Round brush, #3
Script liner, #00

Other Supplies:
Permanent marker, brown
Ruler
Transfer tool

INSTRUCTIONS

Prepare:
1. See Surface Preparation on page 10. Prepare papîer maché boxes. Place lids on boxes.

Paint the Design:
Large Box:
1. Using a ¾" flat brush, paint a 1⅛" wide band around bottom of box with Basil Green. Measure up 1⅛" and paint a second band.

2. Transfer Herb Pots Patterns on page 77 to box sides.

3. See Herb Pots Worksheet on page 78. Paint pots and herbs.

Medium Box:
1. Paint a 1⅛" wide band, 1⅛" up from bottom with Basil Green.

2. Transfer Chives and Tarragon patterns from Herb Pots Patterns on page 77 to box sides.

3. Paint pots and herbs.

Small Box:
1. Paint a 1⅛" wide band around top of box and paint rim of lid with Basil Green.

2. Transfer the Rosemary pattern from Herb Pots Patterns on page 77 to box sides.

3. Paint pots and herbs.

Finish:
1. Using a brown permanent marker, write herb names on bands in ¾" high letters.

2. Using a #00 script liner, paint alongside each ink line with thinned Strawberry Parfait.

3. Ink details with brown permanent marker.

4. Apply matte spray sealer.

Potted Herb Photo Frame

Pictured on page 75

Designed by
Peggy Caldwell

GATHER THESE SUPPLIES

Painting Surfaces:
Papîer maché frame, 8" x 6½", with green/brown gingham design

Paints, Stains, and Finishes:
Acrylic craft paints:
  Basil Green
  Burnt Umber
  Fresh Foliage
  Icy White
  Leaf Green
  Maple Syrup
  Red Violet
  Strawberry Parfait
  Wintergreen
Matte spray sealer
Painting medium:
  extender

Brushes:
Flat brushes, #12, ¾"
Round brush, #3
Script liner, #00

Other Supplies:
Permanent marker, brown
Ruler
Transfer tool

INSTRUCTIONS

Prepare:
1. See Surface Preparation on page 10. Prepare papîer maché frame.

Paint the Design:
1. Using a ¾" flat brush, paint a ¼" band around outer edge of frame and edge of heart opening with Basil Green.

2. Using a #12 flat brush, paint back of frame with Basil Green. Let dry.

3. Transfer Potted Herb Photo Frame Pattern on page 79 onto frame.

4. See Herb Pots Worksheet on page 78. Using Chives description, paint front left herb. Using Rosemary description, paint center herb. Using Oregano description, paint right herb. Let dry.

5. Paint ribbon around center herb.

Finish:
1. Ink details with brown permanent marker.

2. Apply matte spray sealer.

Herb Pots Patterns

Enlarge patterns 122%

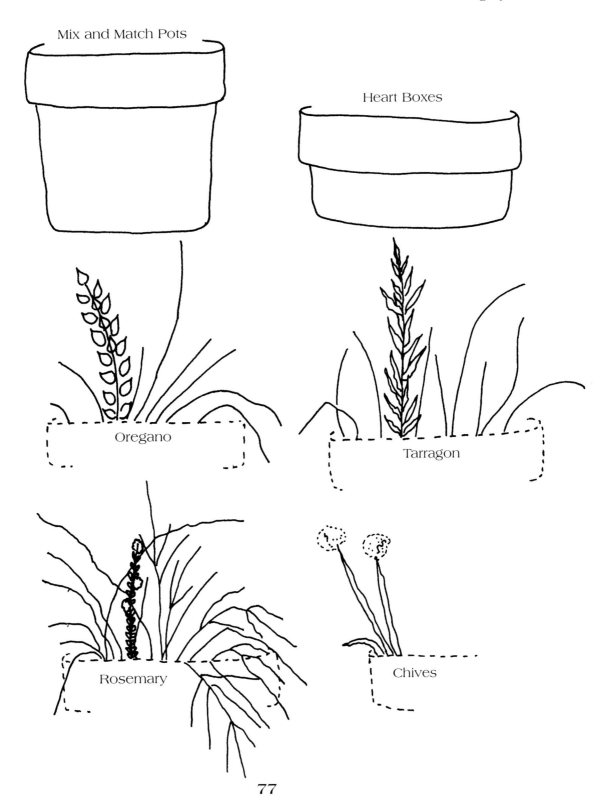

Mix and Match Pots

Heart Boxes

Oregano

Tarragon

Rosemary

Chives

Herb Pots Worksheet

Pot:
Using a #12 flat brush, paint pot with Maple Syrup. Shade with Burnt Umber.

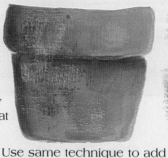

Moss:
Using a #12 flat brush, lay flat and pat with Leaf Green.

Use same technique to add mildew with Icy White.

Chives:
Using a #3 round brush, paint wavy lines with Fresh Foliage, Leaf Green, Wintergreen. Dot flowers with Strawberry Parfait. Highlight with Icy White mixed with Strawberry Parfait.

Herbs

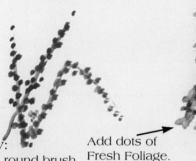

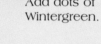

Rosemary:
Using a #3 round brush, paint stems with Leaf Green. Using brush tip, dot leaves over stems.

Add dots of Fresh Foliage.

Add dots of Wintergreen.

Paint rosemary flowers with Icy White mixed with Red Violet.

Oregano:
Using a #3 round brush, paint wavy lines with Leaf Green.

Add dots of Fresh Foliage.

Add dots of Wintergreen.

Tarragon:
Paint leaves and stems with Basil Green mixed with a touch of Icy White and Wintergreen. Use same techniques as chives, using shorter strokes. Highlight with Basil Green mixed with Icy White.

Dirt:
Paint dots of Burnt Umber thinned with extender.

Ribbon:
Using a #00 script liner, paint with thinned Strawberry Parfait.

Potted Herb Photo Frame Pattern

Pattern is actual size

Fill pot with Rosemary.

Fill pot with Chives.

Fill pot with Oregano.

Stenciling Techniques

Stenciling is a decorative technique of applying paint to a surface through cut-out areas of a paint-resistant material to create designs.

Stenciling can decorate almost any surface and can be used to create wonderful flower pots, planters, and window boxes.

SUPPLIES YOU WILL NEED

Stencils:

Precut stencils are durable and reusable and come in a variety of sizes and styles for creating borders and spot motifs. The simplest stencils do not have overlays. Stencils with more than one overlay have printed registration marks on them to be lined up properly.

Some stencils are designed specially for creating backgrounds or creating unique shaped edges that can be used as design elements. They can be used alone or combined with other stencil designs. Stencil blank material is used to create your own designs.

Paints:

Acrylic craft paints and acrylic gloss enamels offer quick drying time and a wide variety of premixed colors. With acrylics, it is easy to mix custom colors to coordinate with home decor. On most surfaces, mistakes can be wiped off before paint dries.

Paint crayons are stencil paints in stick form that are easy to apply and quick and neat to use. They are available individually and in sets.

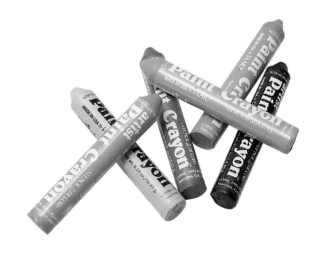

Stencil gels are gel-like stencil paints which produce a translucent, watercolor look. The thick formulation holds well on a brush and can be blended, mixed, and shaded with ease.

Dry brush stencil paints combine quality and convenience. They come in an array of decorator colors and their creamy, no-drip formulation makes them easy to use. They are packaged individually in wide-mouth, palm-size jars or in sets.

Brushes:

Stencil brushes are available in a variety of sizes. To stencil a small, delicate print, choose a ¼" brush; stenciling a large design might require a 1" brush. Choose stencil brushes with densely packed, natural fibers for smooth, soft blending, and solid wood handles. Have a separate brush for each color used in one day. To achieve quality stencil prints, let brush dry thoroughly after cleaning before using it again.

Other Supplies:

• Masking tape - for holding stencils in place

• Paper towels - for blotting brushes and removing seals from dry brush paints and paint crayons

• Disposable plates - to use as paint palettes

• Brush cleaner - for cleaning stencil brushes

SURFACE PREPARATION

Any surface that can be painted or stained can be stenciled. Stenciling can be done over waterbased or oil paints and stains and on gloss, flat, or textured surfaces. They will also adhere to glass if pounced on and wiped gently with a cloth.

When working on a smooth, hard surface, begin stenciling with a light pouncing stroke to build up a thin layer of paint. Let this dry slightly, then go back and shade or darken the edge. If the paint is overworked before the base is dry, the brush will pick up the paint as you try to put it down.

Preparing Clay Pots:

Lightly sand pots and saucers with a flexible sanding sponge to remove sharp edges or rough spots. Use a tack cloth or damp towel to remove dust. Pots and saucers should be clean and dry before stenciling.

Preparing Metal Surfaces:

Very slick, polished metal is not easy to stencil on and paint does not adhere well. Choose, instead, metal containers that come already primed for base-coating, or galvanized or raw metal objects, such as watering cans, buckets, and mailboxes. Be certain the surface is clean and free of dirt and grease.

Galvanized tin has an oily film that must be removed before painting. To wipe it clean, use a sponge and a solution of three parts water to one part vinegar. Dry piece thoroughly before painting. If the metal object will be used out-doors, base-coat with rust resistant paint.

Preparing Wood Surfaces:

Remove wax and dirt before stenciling on wood. If surface is glossy, scuff it up a bit with fine sandpaper to help paint adhere.

New, unfinished wood, or projects that have been stripped and sanded can be stained. If the surface of an unfinished piece is rough, sand in the direction of the grain with fine sandpaper and wipe with a tack cloth. Apply stain according to manufacturer's instructions and let dry.

If stenciling on painted wood, sand piece with extra-fine sandpaper and wipe away dust with a tack cloth. Apply paint to surface, brushing in direction of the grain. Let dry. Buff lightly with a piece of brown paper bag. Apply second coat. Let dry and again buff with paper bag. Repeat if necessary.

If stenciling on new, unfinished pieces sand piece with extra-fine sandpaper and wipe away dust with a tack cloth. Apply paint to surface, brushing in the direction of the grain. Let dry. Buff lightly with a piece of brown paper bag. Apply second coat. Let dry and again buff with paper bag. Repeat if necessary.

SURFACE FINISHING

Since varnishes and polyurethane finishes vary, test the one to be used on a small area of the surface to be stenciled. If the finish causes the stencil paint to blur or bleed, let the test area dry and then lightly mist the project surface with matte spray sealer.

To apply the finishing coat, wipe the entire piece with a tack cloth to remove dust and lint. Use a good quality brush or applicator to apply the finish in direction of the grain. Make certain the finish does not run or puddle. Let dry completely. Wipe piece with a tack cloth. Apply a second coat. Let dry completely. Buff surface with a crumpled brown paper bag. Wipe with a tack cloth. Apply a final finishing coat.

Using Acrylic Craft Paints or Stencil Gels

1 Prepare and paint surface. Let dry. Squeeze a dime-sized amount of acrylic craft paint or stencil gel onto a disposable plate. Group color families for a more efficient blending. Hold stencil brush perpendicular to the disposable plate and pull out a small amount of paint. Twist brush to concentrate paint in center of brush. Try to get most of the paint in center of brush.

2 Swirl brush on a paper towel to remove most of paint. Stenciling is a dry-brushing technique; therefore, most mistakes are made by having too much paint on the brush.

3 Swirl paint onto uncut portion of stencil to determine if you have the right amount of paint. Bring paint into cut-out area with either a light pouncing or circular stroke, keeping brush perpendicular to surface. Use more pressure to shade outside edges or make an opaque print.

Using Paint Crayons

1 Prepare and paint surface. Let dry. A seal automatically forms on the paint crayon when it has not been used for awhile. To remove this seal, gently rub top of crayon on a paper towel.

2 Apply paint crayon to uncut portion of stencil. Never apply paint directly on cut-out area.

3 Using a circular motion, pick up paint from uncut portion of stencil with brush bristles. Work paint to disperse paint evenly through brush bristles. Swirl paint into cut-out areas of stencil, using gentle pressure to avoid buildup of paint along edges.

Using Dry Brush Paints

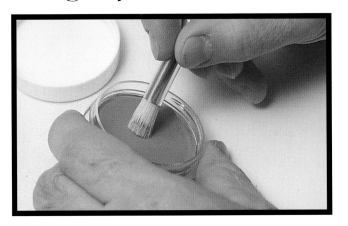

1 Prepare and paint surface. Let dry. Scrape seal from dry brush paint with the handle of your brush. The paint is self-sealing; so it is necessary to remove the seal after each period of inactivity.

2 Swirl brush in paint to load. Swirl brush on uncut portion of stencil to disperse paint evenly through bristles. Do this each time you load the brush.

3 Apply paint in openings of stencil. When working on a smooth, hard surface, begin stenciling with a light pouncing stroke to build up a thin layer of paint. Let this dry slightly; then go back and shade or darken the edge. If paint is overworked before base has dried, the brush will pick up paint as you try to put it down.

Cleaning and Caring for Your Brush

1 Dip the tips of brush bristles into stencil brush cleaner. Activate cleaner by dipping brush in water.

2 Rub brush bristles on the scrubber that is attached to the lid of brush cleaner. Work cleaner into a lather and continue rubbing brush on the scrubber while rinsing it under the tap.

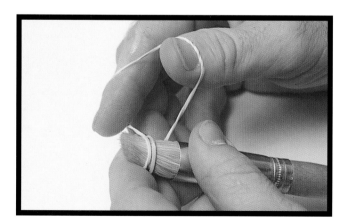

3 Remove excess water from brush bristles. Place rubber band around brush bristles. Let brush dry on its side. Store flat or with bristles up--never store a brush with bristles down or bent.

Cutting Your Own Stencils

SUPPLIES YOU WILL NEED

- Craft knife, sharp

- Glass cutting board, ⅜" or ½" thick with ground or sanded edges (available at a glass shop)

- Permanent fine tip marker (A regular ballpoint or felt tip pen will not write on stencil material.)

- Stencil blank material

- White paper to fit under glass

- *Optional:* Electric stencil cutting tool

Tips:
- Cut small intricate shapes first. Try to cut shape without lifting blade from stencil blank material. Use sufficient pressure to cut through stencil material with one stroke---preventing a jagged edge. The cut edge is the edge to be painted.

2 Using a sharp craft knife, cut out open areas of the design. Move the stencil blank material as you cut, rather than moving the knife.

1 Place stencil blank material over desired pattern. Trace pattern onto stencil blank material with permanent marker. Place white paper under glass. Place stencil blank material on glass cutting board.

3 *Optional method for cutting:* Place white paper under glass. Place stencil blank material on glass cutting board. Using an electric stencil cutting tool, cut out open areas of the design.

English Topiary Floorcloth
Instructions begin on page 89

English Topiary Floorcloth

Pictured on page 88

Designed by
Kathi Malarchuk

GATHER THESE SUPPLIES

Stenciling Surface:
Vinyl flooring remnant,
   28" x 42"

Paints, Stains, and Finishes:
Acrylic craft paint:
   Bayberry
Colored glazes:
   Bark Brown
   Deep Woods Green
   Ivy Green
   Pompeii Red
   Russet
   White
Flat paint or gesso:
   White
Glazing medium:
   Neutral
Satin finish urethane

Brushes:
Flat brush, #12
Round brush, #3
Stencil brush

Other Supplies:
Brown paper bags, clean
Disappearing marker
Disposable plates
Masking tape, 1"
Plastic wrap
Printing blocks design: Ivy
Ruler
Stencil: Pots & Planters

INSTRUCTIONS

Prepare:
1. Using a #12 flat brush, base-coat back of vinyl flooring remnant with two coats White paint or gesso. Let dry between coats.

2. Paint over base-coat with two coats Bayberry. Let dry between coats.

3. Mix two parts White colored glaze with one part Neutral glazing medium. Pour onto disposable plate. Crumple a 12" square of plastic wrap. Dip crumpled plastic wrap in glaze mixture. Pat glaze lightly over entire surface of vinyl, creating a mottled look. Let dry 24 hours.

4. Mask off a 4" border on all sides. Using a #12 flat brush, work one small section at a time and brush border with Deep Woods Green Glaze. Crumple a 12" square of plastic wrap. Pat crumpled plastic wrap over glaze to remove some glaze, creating a mottled look. Repeat until entire border has been mottled. Remove tape. Let dry.

Stencil the Design:
1. See Stenciling Techniques on pages 80-87. Using small pot stencil on the Pots & Planters stencil, stencil three pots in center area of floorcloth with Russet, using photo on page 88 as a guide.

2. Shade with Pompeii Red.

Block Print the Design:
1. Using disappearing marker, draw shapes of heart for center topiary and circles for left and right topiaries.

2. See Block Printing Techniques on pages 97-100. Block print ivy leaves for topiaries with Deep Woods Green and Ivy Green.

3. Using a #3 round brush, paint twining stems, vines, and tendrils with a mixture of Bark Brown and Neutral Glazes. Let dry 72 hours.

Finish:
1. Apply 3-5 coats satin finish urethane. Let dry and buff between coats with pieces cut from clean brown paper bags.

Beribboned Clay Pot

Pictured on page 90

Designed by
Kathi Malarchuk

GATHER THESE SUPPLIES

Stenciling Surface:
Clay pot, 10" dia.

Paints, Stains, and Finishes:
Acrylic craft paint:
   Tapioca
Acrylic stencil gel:
   Berry Red
Blending gel medium
Découpage medium
Matte spray sealer

Brushes:
Old toothbrush
Sponge brush, 1"
Stencil brush

Other Supplies:
Stencil: Ribbon & Bow

INSTRUCTIONS

Prepare:
1. See Surface Preparation on page 82. Prepare clay pot.
Continued on page 91

Beribboned Clay Pot
Instructions begin on page 89

Ivy Checkerboard Tin Planter
Instructions begin on page 91

Birds & Blossoms Wooden Planter
Instructions begin on page 91

Continued from page 89

2. Using a 1" sponge brush, seal pot inside and out with découpage medium. Let dry.

3. Base-coat pot with 2 coats of Tapioca.

4. Paint rim of pot with Berry Red.

5. Using an old toothbrush, spatter rim with Tapioca.

Stencil the Design:
1. See Stenciling Techniques on pages 80-87. Using the Ribbon & Bow stencil, stencil ribbon and bow around pot with Berry Red mixed with blending gel medium for background and Berry Red for horizontal and vertical stripes that form the plaid. Use photo on page 90 as a guide. Let dry.

Finish:
1. Apply matte spray sealer.

Ivy Checkerboard Tin Planter

Pictured on page 90

Designed by
Jane Gauss

GATHER THESE SUPPLIES

Stenciling Surface:
Oval galvanized tin planter

Paints, Stains, and Finishes:
Stencil gels:
  Cactus
  Twig
  White
  Wild Ivy
Matte spray sealer
Optional: Exterior waterbase
  varnish

Brushes:
Stencil brush

Other Supplies:
Stencils:
  Checkerboard Background
  Ivy

INSTRUCTIONS

Prepare:
1. See Surface Preparation on page 82. Prepare tin planter.

Stencil the Design:
1. See Stenciling Techniques on pages 80-87. Using the Checkerboard Background stencil, stencil checkerboard around sides of planter with White. Use photo on page 90 as a guide. Let dry.

2. Using Ivy stencil, stencil ivy with Wild Ivy. Stencil leaves with Cactus and Wild Ivy. Stencil leaf veins and vines with Twig. Let dry.

Finish:
1. Apply matte spray sealer.

Optional: If planter is to be used outdoors, apply 2 to 3 coats exterior waterbase varnish to inside and outside of planter.

Birds & Blossoms Wooden Planter

Pictured on page 90

Designed by
Lisa Moon

GATHER THESE SUPPLIES

Stenciling Surface:
Unfinished wood planter

Paints, Stains, and Finishes:
Stencil gels:
  Daffodil Yellow
  Deep Purple
  Ivory Lace
  Pumpkin
  Teal Bayou
  Tempest Blue
  Twig
  Wild Ivy
  Wood Rose
Antiquing medium:
  Honey Gold
Matte spray sealer
Varnish or polyurethane finish

Brushes:
Sponge brush, 1"
Stencil brush

Other Supplies:
Sandpaper, 220 grit
Soft cloths
Stencil: Apple Blossoms
  & Bird's Nest

INSTRUCTIONS

Prepare:
1. See Surface Preparation on page 82. Prepare wood planter.

2. Using a soft cloth, antique planter with Honey Gold. Let dry.

Stencil:

1. See Stenciling Techniques on pages 80-87. Using Apple Blossoms & Bird's Nest stencil, stencil branches onto front of planter with Twig, flowers and buds with Wood Rose, flower shading with Deep Purple, flower centers with Daffodil Yellow, and leaves with Wild Ivy.

2. Stencil body of chickadee onto branch with Daffodil Yellow; wings, tail, and head with Tempest Blue; legs with Pumpkin.

3. Stencil body of nesting bird with Ivory Lace, feathers on second and third overlays with Teal Bayou, branches and leaves with Wild Ivy and Twig. Let dry.

Finish:

1. Apply matte spray sealer. Let dry.

2. Using a 1" sponge brush, apply several coats varnish or polyurethane.

Roses Go Round Pots

Pictured on page 93

Designed by Alma Lynne

GATHER THESE SUPPLIES

Painting Surfaces:
Clay pot, 9" dia.
Clay pot, 6" dia.

Paints, Stains, and Finishes:
Acrylic craft paints:
  Engine Red
  True Blue
  Wicker White
  Yellow Light
Matte spray sealer

Brushes:
Sponge brush, 1"
Stencil brush

Other Supplies:
Craft knife
Glass or other cutting surface
Permanent marker, fine-tip
Stencil blank material
Transfer tool

INSTRUCTIONS

Prepare:
1. See Surface Preparation on page 82. Prepare clay pots.

2. Using a 1" sponge brush, base-coat rim of 9" clay pot and base of 6" clay pot with Wicker White. Let dry.

3. Transfer Roses Go Round Pots Pattern to rim of 9" clay pot and base of 6" clay pot.

Cut the Stencil:
1. See Cutting Your Own Stencils on page 87. Transfer Roses Go Round Pots Pattern to stencil blank material.

2. Using a craft knife, cut out stencil.

Stencil the Design:
1. Stencil flowers around large pot with True Blue.

2. Stencil flowers around small pot with Engine Red, True Blue, and Yellow Light. Let dry.

Finish:
1. Apply matte spray sealer.

Roses Go Round Pots Pattern

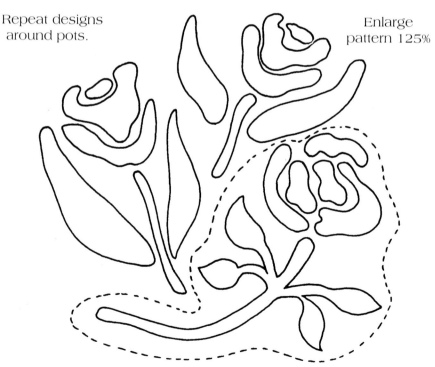

Repeat designs around pots.

Enlarge pattern 125%

Use pattern inside dotted line around rim of large pot.

Roses Go Round Pots
Instructions begin
on page 92

Fern House Sign
Instructions begin
on page 95

9373

Picket Fence
Planter
Instructions begin
on page 95

Sponged
Pot
Instructions
begin
on page 96

Plaid Pot
Instructions begin
on page 96

Picket Fence Planter

Pictured on page 94

Designed by
Susan Goans Driggers

GATHER THESE SUPPLIES

Painting Surfaces:
Pine, 1" x 6", 6½' long;
    1" x 1", 4' long
Wooden stakes with pointed
    ends (11)

Paints, Stains, and Finishes:
Acrylic craft paints:
    Meadow Green
    Nutmeg
    Peach Perfection
    Wicker White

Brushes:
Sponge brush, 1"
Stencil brush

Other Supplies:
Clay pots, 4" dia. (4)
Craft knife
Disposable plate
Fern frond
Hand saw
Measuring tape
Natural sponge
Sandpaper
Screwdriver
Stencil blank material
Wood screws

INSTRUCTIONS

Prepare:
1. Using a hand saw, cut the
1" x 6" board into five pieces:
three 22" long and two 6"
long. Cut two pieces from the
1" x 1" board, each 22" long.

2. Construct box with wood
screws, using 22" boards for
sides and bottom and 6"
boards for ends.

3. See Surface Preparation on
page 82. Prepare wood box.

4. Using a 1" sponge brush,
base-coat outside of box with
Wicker White.

5. Base-coat inside of box
with Meadow Green.

6. Base-coat 1" x 1" pieces
and 11 stakes with Wicker
White.

7. Place 1" x 1" pieces parallel
on work surface, several
inches apart. Position stakes
along 1" x 1" to create picket
fence. Screw pickets in place.
Base-coat again with Wicker
White. Let dry.

8. Screw picket fence to back
of box.

Paint the Design:
1. See How to Sponge on
page 112. Dampen natural
sponge with water. Squeeze
out excess water.

2. Squeeze some Peach
Perfection paint onto a
disposable plate. Rub and
bounce one side of sponge in
paint on plate, be certain
sponge has soaked paint into
surface and is saturated.

3. Press paint-filled side of
sponge on lower edges of
planter and pickets.

4. Rinse sponge. Squeeze out
excess water. Sponge lower
edges of planter and pickets
with Nutmeg. Let dry.

Stencil the Design:
1. See Cutting Your Own
Stencils on page 87. Using a
fern frond as a pattern, make
a fern stencil.

2. Stencil ferns randomly and
lightly onto front of planter
with Meadow Green. Let dry.

Finish:
1. Place 4" clay pots inside
wooden planter.

Fern House Sign

Pictured on page 94

Designed by
Susan Goans Driggers

GATHER THESE SUPPLIES

Painting surface:
Wooden sign with curved
    ends
Wooden house numbers

Paints, Stains, and Finishes:
Acrylic craft paints:
    Forest Green
    Meadow Green
    Nutmeg
    Peach Perfection
    Wicker White

Brushes:
Sponge brush, 1"
Stencil brush

Other Supplies:
Fern frond
Masking tape
Stencil blank material
Wood glue

INSTRUCTIONS

Prepare:
1. See Surface Preparation on page 82. Prepare wood sign and numbers.

2. Using a 1" sponge brush, base-coat sign with Wicker White.

3. Paint inner edge of sign rim and numbers with Forest Green. Paint outer edge of rim with Nutmeg. Let dry.

Stencil the Design:
1. See Cutting Your Own Stencils on page 87. Using a fern frond, make a fern stencil.

2. Stencil ferns randomly on bottom edge of sign with Meadow Green. Let dry.

3. Using masking tape, section off blocks on sign to frame house numbers.

4. Using a 1" sponge brush, paint inside masked-off sections with Peach Perfection and Nutmeg. Do not blend paint. Let dry. Remove tape.

Finish:
1. Using wood glue, attach numbers inside painted blocks.

Sponged Pot

Pictured on page 94

Designed by
Susan Goans Driggers

GATHER THESE SUPPLIES

Painting Surface:
Clay pot, 8" dia.

Paints, Stains, and Finishes:
Acrylic craft paints:
Forest Green
Meadow Green
Nutmeg
Peach Perfection
Wicker White
Matte spray sealer

Brushes:
Sponge brush, 1"

Other Supplies:
Natural sponge

INSTRUCTIONS

Prepare:
1. See Surface Preparation on page 82. Prepare clay pot.

2. Using a 1" sponge brush, base-coat with Wicker White. Let dry.

Paint the Design:
1. See How to Sponge on page 112. Using a natural sponge, sponge bottom section of pot with Peach Perfection. Sponge again with Nutmeg.

2. Sponge top section of pot with Forest Green. Sponge again with Meadow Green.

Finish:
1. Apply matte spray sealer.

Plaid Pot

Pictured on page 94

Designed by
Susan Goans Driggers

GATHER THESE SUPPLIES

Painting Surface:
Clay pot, 8" dia.

Paints, Stains, and Finishes:
Acrylic craft paints:
Forest Green
Meadow Green
Nutmeg
Peach Perfection
Wicker White
Matte spray sealer

Brushes:
Sponge brush, 1"

Other Supplies:
Cellulose sponge
Disposable plate

INSTRUCTIONS

Prepare:
1. See Surface Preparations on page 82. Prepare clay pot.

2. Using a 1" sponge brush, base-coat pot with Wicker White. Let dry.

Paint the Design:
1. See How to Sponge on page 112. Dampen cellulose sponge and squeeze out excess water. Squeeze dime-sized amount of Forest Green onto disposable plate. Level paint in plate. Dip side of sponge in paint. Press sponge to pot surface, creating vertical stripes. Use photo on page 94 as a guide.

2. Rinse sponge. Repeat sponging with Meadow Green, Nutmeg, and Peach Perfection. Let dry.

3. Add sponged horizontal stripes in same colors to create plaid.

Finish:
1. Apply matte spray sealer.

Block Printing Techniques

Block printing uses cutout shapes made of a flexible foam material to create stamped designs on surfaces. It's simple to learn and fun to do.

SET UP WORK SURFACE

Set up work area on a sturdy table covered with paper or plastic. If working with many printing blocks, have a container of water with a drop of mild dish soap in it nearby for cleaning blocks as you work. Have brushes handy. One flat brush can be used to load printing blocks with several colors of paint. When changing to another color family, swish brush in water, then blot it dry on an old towel.

SUPPLIES YOU WILL NEED

Printing Blocks:
Printing blocks are available in a wide range of precut designs. There are designs available for every decorating style, as well as blank block materials for cutting your own designs.

Printing blocks are die-cut from a soft and durable stamping material that is easy to clean and can be used time and time again. Each block has its own handle that makes loading and setting the block onto the surface easier. Because they are flexible, you can use printing blocks around corners and rounded surfaces.

Paint and Colored Glazes:
Available in a wide array of colors, paint glazes have a subtle transparency and a gel-like consistency. Acrylic craft paints mixed with a glazing medium, painting medium, or paint conditioner can also be used for block printing.

Brushes:
Load blocks with a flat brush. Though one brush can be used for several like colors, have two or three loading brushes available.

Use a pointed, round brush to add vines, tendrils, and stems to block-printed designs.

Other Supplies:

- Brown paper bag for blotting loaded blocks

- Hand towel, slightly-moistened for correcting mistakes

- Old towel for drying brushes and hands

- Practice paper

- Soft toothbrush for cleaning blocks

- Water for cleaning brushes and blocks

SURFACE PREPARATION

Preparing Clay Pots:

Seal surface of clean, dry pot with two coats of découpage finish. You may block-print on clay surface or base-coat with acrylic craft paint.

Use a liner for plants or seal inside of pot with two coats of découpage finish, so moisture won't seep through and ruin block design.

Apply a urethane finish after block printing has dried, if pot is to be used outdoors.

Preparing Plaster and Unglazed Ceramics:

Most glazed surfaces are slick, so loaded blocks tend to slide. To prevent slippage, lightly spray surface with a matte spray sealer. When block printing is dry, spray with several coats of sealer. Block-printed, glazed ceramic pieces are best used for decorative purposes. The block-printed designs will not stand up to heavy wear and frequent washing.

Preparing Wood Surfaces:

Remove wax and dirt before blocking on wood. If surface is glossy or rough, scuff with fine sandpaper to help paint adhere.

Wood projects can be stained before blocking. If surface is rough, sand in direction of the grain with fine sandpaper and wipe with a tack cloth. Apply stain or acrylic craft paint, according to manufacturer's instructions. Let dry.

CLEAN UP

To prevent build-up of glaze, toss blocks not currently in use into a bucket of water. Periodically clean blocks used for many pressings to produce better prints. When ready to use that shape again, blot firmly on old towel and load.

When finished for the day, put blocks into warm water with mild dish soap. Scrub each with a soft toothbrush or cellulose sponge, gently opening cuts to remove built-up glaze. Rinse and blot with towel. Wash glaze from flat brushes until rinse water is clean. Shape bristles and store flat.

CORRECTING MISTAKES

Mistakes can be minimized by cutting a piece of paper the size of project surface and using it to practice placement of designs. Use the project photo as a guide for design and color placement.

If too much glaze goes on the block and it slides on the surface, here are some options:

- Remove smudged print that has not dried by whisking it away with slightly moistened corner of an old towel. If glaze has stained surface, re-block in the same place.

- Because glazes do not dry instantly, a smudged print can most often be saved and redefined. Press another two or three prints with loaded block to use up some of the glaze. Then go back to first print, reposition block over smudged print, and press again.

- Clean up edge of a slightly smudged print. If there is a fingerprint or smudge from glaze on the handle, use a slightly dampened cotton swab to clean up edge of shape.

- Turn a mistake into part of design by printing another leaf or shape over mistake.

Applying Printing Blocks

1 Squeeze dime-sized amount of paint onto a disposable plate. Dip flat brush in water and blot on a paper towel to remove excess water. Load brush with paint. Hold block by handle and apply thin coat of paint to cut side. Do not get paint on handle. Brush paint out to edge.

3 Holding loaded block by the handle, place on project surface. Use other hand to gently press block against surface without sliding it. Release handle as soon as block touches surface to avoid sliding block.

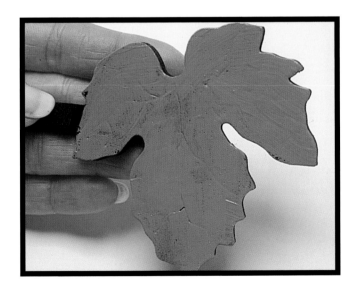

2 More than one color can be added to each block. If a particular design has a flower and a leaf on one block, simply apply green to leaf area and another color to flower area.

4 Use fingertips to press block. While one hand gently holds block let other fingers walk around block. Using handle, lift block. Move to another section and repeat process. Make 2 or 3 prints before applying more paint.

Cutting Your Own Printing Block

1 Choose a simple, silhouette-type design. Trace design with sharp lead pencil onto tracing vellum. You can also use actual leaves or flowers by pressing them and placing them on a copy machine to reduce or enlarge as desired. Trace design onto tracing vellum. In either case, make certain you add a handle to design.

To cut outer edge, place printing block material on glass. Place pattern over printing block material and secure with tape. Use very sharp craft knife to cut through pattern into pad.

2 On straight edges, make a clean, straight cut all the way through pad. Keep side of blade flush against pattern. Do not angle blade. Achieve a straight up-and-down cut. On curved edges, use a sawing motion to cut about halfway through at the points and turns, lift blade and reposition it. Do not try to rotate material with blade in position.

3 To cut veins and details, hold pattern to surface and cut through tracing. Cut halfway through printing block material following detail markings. Be careful not to cut completely through pad. Remove tracing.

Test block before working on actual project. If there are ragged edges, put a new blade into craft knife and carefully trim ragged edges away.

Tulip Pots
Instructions begin on page 102

Tulip Pots

Pictured on page 101

Designed by
Lisa Moon & Karen Reif

GATHER THESE SUPPLIES

Block Printing Surfaces:
Clay pot, 10" dia
Clay pot, 4" dia.

Paints, Stains, and Finishes:
Acrylic craft paints:
 Thicket
 Wicker White
Metallic acrylic craft paints:
 Antique Gold
Colored glazes:
 Baby Pink
 Geranium Red
 Ivy Green
 New Leaf Green
 Sage Green
 Sunflower
 Vibrant Pink
Matte spray sealer

Brushes:
Old toothbrush
Sponge brush, 1"

Other Supplies:
Printing block: Tulips

INSTRUCTIONS

Prepare:
1. See Surface Preparation on page 98. Prepare clay pots.

2. Using a 1" sponge brush, base-coat lower parts of pots with Wicker White.

3. Paint rims of pots with Thicket. Let dry.

Block-Print the Design:
1. See Block Printing Techniques on pages 97-100. Using the Tulips printing block, block-print leaves with Ivy Green, New Leaf Green, and Sage Green around sides of pots. Use photo on page 101 as a guide.

2. Block-print tulips with Baby Pink, Geranium Red, Sunflower, and Vibrant Pink.

Finish:
1. Using a 1" sponge brush, paint rims of pots with Antique Gold.

2. Dilute Antique Gold paint with water, using half water and half paint. Using an old toothbrush, spatter sides of pots with diluted paint. Let dry.

3. Apply matte spray sealer.

Miniature Fruits Pot

Pictured on page 103

Designed by
Lisa Moon

GATHER THESE SUPPLIES

Block Printing Surface:
Clay pot, 8" dia.

Paints, Stains, and Finishes:
Acrylic craft paints:
 Lavender Sachet
 Wicker White
Colored glazes:
 Bark Brown
 Black Cherry
 Deep Purple
 Geranium Red
 Ivy Green
 Lemon Yellow
 Neutral
 New Leaf Green
 Persimmon
 Sage Green
Matte spray sealer

Brushes:
Round brush, #3
Sponge brush, 1"

Other Supplies:
Natural sponge
Printing block: Mini Fruits

INSTRUCTIONS

Prepare:
1. See Surface Preparation on page 98. Prepare clay pot.

2. Using a 1" sponge brush, base-coat pot with Lavender Sachet.

3. Mix equal amounts Wicker White and Neutral. Brush on pot. Wipe off excess with a natural sponge. Let dry.

Block-Print the Design:
1. See Block Printing Techniques on pages 97-100. Using the Mini Fruits printing block, block-print leaves with Ivy Green, New Leaf Green, and Sage Green. Use Miniature Fruits Pot Pattern on page 104 as a guide.

2. Block-print apples with Black Cherry, Geranium Red, and Lemon Yellow.

3. Block-print pears with Lemon Yellow, New Leaf Green, and Persimmon.

Continued on page 104

Grapevine Pot
Instructions begin
on page 104

Miniature Fruits Pot
Instructions begin
on page 102

Continued from page 102

4. Block-print grapes with Deep Purple and New Leaf Green.

5. Block-print peaches with Persimmon.

Finish:
1. Using a #3 round brush, paint vines and stems with Bark Brown, New Leaf Green, and Sage Green. Let dry.

2. Apply matte spray sealer.

Grapevine Pot

Pictured on page 103

Designed by
Lisa Moon

GATHER THESE SUPPLIES

Block Printing Surface:
Clay pot, 10" dia.

Paints, Stains, and Finishes:
Acrylic craft paint:
  Wicker White
Colored glazes:
  Deep Purple
  Deep Woods Green
  Ivy Green
Antiquing medium:
  Woodn' Bucket Brown
Gloss spray sealer

Brushes:
Round brush, #3
Sponge brushes, 1" (2)

Other Supplies:
Cellulose sponge
Printing block: Grape Vine

INSTRUCTIONS

Prepare:
1. See Surface Preparation on page 98. Prepare clay pot.

2. Using a 1" sponge brush, base-coat pot with Wicker White. Apply 2 to 3 coats. Let dry.

Block-Print the Design:
1. See Block Printing Techniques on pages 97-100. Using the Grape Vine printing block, block-print grapes around sides of pot with Deep Purple. Use photo on page 103 as a guide.

2. Block-print leaves with Deep Woods Green and Ivy Green.

3. Using a #3 round brush, paint vines and stems with Ivy Green. Let dry.

4. Using a 1" sponge brush, apply Woodn' Bucket Brown to pot.

5. Dampen cellulose sponge. Squeeze out excess water. Rub surface of pot to remove excess antiquing medium, leaving enough to create a mellow, aged look. Let dry.

Finish:
1. Apply gloss spray sealer.

Miniature Fruits Pot Pattern

Enlarge pattern 375%

Flowers & Butterflies Planter

Pictured on pages 106 & 107

Designed by
Lisa Moon

GATHER THESE SUPPLIES

Block Printing Surface:
Wooden planter,
23½" x 7", 5½" tall

Paints, Stains, and Finishes:
Acrylic craft paint:
  Wicker White
Colored glazes:
  Baby Pink
  Bark Brown
  Blue Bell
  Danish Blue
  Deep Purple
  Geranium Red
  Ivy Green
  New Leaf Green
  Sage Green
  Sunflower
  Vibrant Pink
Matte spray sealer

Brushes:
Round brush, #3
Sponge brush, 2"

Other Supplies:
Printing blocks:
  Critters
  Little Garden Flowers

INSTRUCTIONS

Prepare:
1. See Surface Preparation on page 98. Prepare wooden planter.

2. Dilute Wicker White with water, half water and half paint. Using a 2" sponge brush, base-coat box with diluted paint. Let dry.

Block Print the Design:
1. See Block-Printing Techniques on pages 97-100. Using Critters and Little Garden Flowers printing blocks, block-print flowers with Baby Pink, Blue Bell, Danish Blue, Deep Purple, Geranium Red, Sunflower, and Vibrant Pink. Use Flowers & Butterflies Planter Pattern as guide.

2. Block-print leaves Ivy Green, New Leaf Green, and Sage Green.

3. Block-print butterflies with Blue Bell, Danish Blue, Deep Purple, and Sunflower.

4. Using a #3 round brush, paint vines with Sage Green and stems with Bark Brown. Let dry.

Finish:
1. Apply matte spray sealer.

Flowers & Butterflies Planter Pattern

Enlarge pattern 235%

Flowers & Butterflies
Planter
Instructions begin on page 105

Crackle Techniques

Crackle medium reproduces a weathered-paint look, adding age and character instantly.

SUPPLIES YOU WILL NEED

Paints, Stains, and Finishes:
Acrylic craft paint
Crackle medium
Matte spray sealer
Waterbase varnish

Brushes:
Sponge brush

Other Supplies:
Cellulose sponge
Sandpaper, extra-fine grit
Tack cloth

SURFACE PREPARATION

Preparing Clay Pots:
Sand rough areas on pots and saucers with extra-fine grit sandpaper. Using a tack cloth, wipe away dust.

HOW TO CRACKLE

1. Using a sponge brush, base-coat surface with acrylic craft paint.

2. Apply a smooth coat of crackle medium.

3. Apply varnish over the crackle medium, leveling out each long stroke. Work quickly – covering, but not overlapping. A thick coat will make larger, wider cracks; a thin coat will make thin cracks. The crackle effect appears instantly, but over-brushing will make it disappear.

4. Let dry, at least 24 hours.

5. Squeeze dime-sized amount of paint on one side of a damp cellulose sponge. Squeeze to fill cellulose sponge. Rub paint onto surface of project and into cracks. Remove excess by rubbing while paint is still damp until reaching desired results. Let dry.

6. Apply matte spray sealer.

Crackled Cherub Pot

Pictured on page 109

Designed by
Susan Goans Driggers

GATHER THESE SUPPLIES

Painting Surface:
Clay pot with cherubs, 7" dia.

Paints, Stains, and Finishes:
Acrylic craft paints:
  Antique Gold
  Emerald Green
  Ice Blue
Crackle medium
Matte spray sealer
Waterbase varnish

Brushes:
Sponge brush, 1"

Other Supplies:
Cellulose sponge

INSTRUCTIONS

Prepare:
1. See Surface Preparation above. Prepare clay pot.

Paint the Design:
1. Using a 1" sponge brush, base-coat outer bottom of pot with Antique Gold. Paint outer top rim and cherubs with Ice Blue. Paint interior with Emerald Green. Let dry.

Crackle the Design:
1. See How to Crackle above. Apply crackle medium. Let dry.

2. Apply waterbase varnish.

3. Dilute Antique Gold with water and using a cellulose sponge rub over surface cracks in areas painted with Emerald Green and Ice Blue. Dilute Ice Blue and rub over cracks in areas painted with Antique Gold.

Finish:
1. Apply matte spray sealer.

Crackled Cherub Pot
Instructions begin on page 108

Antiquing Techniques

Acrylic craft paints can be mixed with a neutral glazing medium to make a glaze mixture for antiquing. The glaze mixture allows the base color to show through and creates subtle highlights.

SUPPLIES YOU WILL NEED

Paints, Stains, and Finishes:
Acrylic craft paint
Glazing medium
Matte spray sealer

Brushes:
Deerfoot brush
Sponge brush

Other Supplies:
Cellulose sponge
Disposable plate

HOW TO ANTIQUE

1. *Optional:* Using a sponge brush, base-coat project with one color of acrylic craft paint. Let dry.

2. Mix equal amounts of another color of acrylic craft paint and glazing medium. Pour a small amount of mixture onto a disposable plate.

3. Using a deerfoot brush, apply glaze mixture to surface forcing glaze in all small crevices.

4. Dampen the cellulose sponge and squeeze out excess water. Rub project surface with cellulose sponge to remove excess glaze mixture, leaving as much as desired. Let dry.

5. Apply matte spray sealer.

Ivy Planter

Pictured on page 111

Designed by
Susan Goans Driggers

GATHER THESE SUPPLIES

Painting Surface:
Clay planter, with raised ivy
  motif, 5" tall

Paints, Stains, and Finishes:
Acrylic craft paint:
  Hunter Green
Glazing medium:
  Neutral
Matte spray sealer

Brushes:
Deerfoot brush
Sponge brush, 1"

Other Supplies:
Cellulose sponge
Disposable plate

INSTRUCTIONS

Prepare:
1. See Surface Preparation on page 9. Prepare clay pot.

Antique the Design:
1. See How to Antique above. Mix equal amounts Hunter Green and Neutral. Using a 1" sponge brush, base-coat planter with mixture.

2. Using a deerfoot brush, apply glaze mixture to surface, forcing glaze in small crevices and raised design areas.

3. Dampen cellulose sponge and squeeze out excess water. Rub pot surface with sponge to remove excess glaze mixture. Let dry.

Finish:
1. Apply matte spray sealer.

Swag Motif Flower Pot

Pictured on page 111

Designed by
Susan Goans Driggers

GATHER THESE SUPPLIES

Painting Surface:
Clay pot, with raised swag
  motif, 6" dia.

Continued on page 112

Swag Motif Flower Pot
Instructions begin on page 110

Ivy Planter
Instructions begin
on page 110

Continued from page 110

Paints, Stains, and Finishes:
Acrylic craft paints:
  Amish Blue
  Charcoal Grey
Glazing medium:
  Neutral
Matte spray sealer

Brushes:
Deerfoot brush
Sponge brush, 1"

Other Supplies:
Cellulose sponge
Disposable plate

INSTRUCTIONS

Prepare:
1. See Surface Preparation on page 9. Prepare clay pot.

2. Using a 1" sponge brush, base-coat pot with Charcoal Grey. Let dry.

Antique the Design:
1. See How to Antique on page 110. Using a 1" sponge brush, base-coat surface with Amish Blue and Neutral.

2. Using a deerfoot brush, apply mixture to pot, forcing mixture in small crevices on design area.

3. Dampen cellulose sponge. Squeeze out excess water. Rub pot to remove excess mixture. Let dry.

Finish:
1. Apply matte spray sealer.

Sponging Techniques

Sponging creates soft, light, airy effects and adds subtle, cloud-like interest to painted surfaces. The base color shows through, producing a beautiful effect in one simple step.

SUPPLIES YOU WILL NEED

Paints, Stains, and Finishes:
Acrylic craft paint

Other Supplies:
Compressed sponge
Craft knife or scissors
Cutting mat
Disposable plate
Dry cloth, clean

HOW TO SPONGE

1. Dampen sponge with water. Squeeze sponge or press it against a clean, dry cloth to remove excess water.

2. Squeeze acrylic craft paint onto disposable plate. Rub and bounce one side of the sponge in paint. Be certain sponge has soaked up paint and is saturated.

3. Gently press paint-filled side of sponge on project surface. Do not smear or rub; press

lightly and pick directly up.

4. Repeat until surface is covered with desired amount of sponging.

5. To sponge various shapes onto your item, a sponge can be cut into shapes, such as squares, hearts, etc. Cut shapes with a craft knife on a cutting mat before wetting sponge.

112

Sunflower Pot

Pictured on page 114

Designed by
Susan Goans Driggers

GATHER THESE SUPPLIES

Painting Surface:
Clay pot, 7" dia.

Paints, Stains, and Finishes:
Acrylic craft paints:
  Buttercup
  Cinnamon
  Poetry Green
  Wicker White
Matte spray sealer

Brushes:
Flat brush, #6
Liner, #00

Other Supplies:
Natural sponge
Rub-on transfers: Sunflowers
Pencil

INSTRUCTIONS

Prepare:
1. See Surface Preparation on page 9. Prepare clay pot.

2. Using a #6 flat brush, base-coat pot with Wicker White.

3. Lightly pencil a line around pot for placement of sunflowers transfer, using photo on page 114 as a guide.

Paint the Design:
1. See How to Sponge on page 112. Sponge pot below pencil line with Cinnamon.

2. Make vertical strokes to form stripes around rim of pot with diluted Buttercup.

3. Using a #00 liner, outline stripes with Poetry Green.

Finish:
1. Apply Sunflowers rub-on transfers following manufacturer's instructions.

2. Apply matte spray sealer.

Violets Découpage Pot

Pictured on page 114

Designed by
Susan Goans Driggers

GATHER THESE SUPPLIES

Painting Surface:
Clay pot, 7" dia.

Paints, Stains, and Finishes:
Acrylic craft paints:
  Burnt Umber
  Fresh Foliage
  Poetry Green
  Southern Pine
Découpage medium

Other Supplies:
Natural sponge
Paper with violet motifs
Scissors

INSTRUCTIONS

Prepare:
1. See Surface Preparation on page 9. Prepare clay pot.

Paint the Design:
1. See How to Sponge on page 112. To create moss appearance, lightly sponge each paint color on pot, overlapping in some areas. Let clay show in other areas.

Finish:
1. Cut out violet motifs from paper. Using découpage medium, glue motifs to pot. Let dry.

2. Apply additional coats of découpage medium. Let dry between coats.

Rose Pot

Pictured on page 115

Designed by
Susan Goans Driggers

GATHER THESE SUPPLIES

Painting Surface:
Clay pot, 10" dia.

Paints, Stains, and Finishes:
Acrylic craft paints:
  Poetry Green
  Wicker White
Matte spray sealer

Brushes:
Sponge brush, 1"

Other Supplies:
Cellulose sponge
Craft knife
Rub-on transfers: Roses

INSTRUCTIONS

Prepare:
1. See Surface Preparation on page 9. Prepare clay pot.

2. Using a 1" sponge brush, base-coat pot with Wicker White. Let dry.

Paint the Design:
1. See How to Sponge on page 112. Using a craft knife, cut sponge in squares so two

Continued on page 116

Violets Découpage Pot
Instructions begin on page 113

Sunflower Pot
Instructions begin
on page 113

Rose Pot
Instructions begin
on page 113

Pansy Pot
Instructions begin on page 116

Continued from page 113

squares will fit the height of the pot.

2. Sponge upper and lower edges of rim of pot with Poetry Green.

3. Sponge checks on lower area of pot by pressing sponge square in paint then pressing on surface. Lift.

Finish:
1. Apply Roses rub-on transfers, following manufacturer's instructions.

2. Apply matte spray sealer.

Pansy Pot

Pictured on page 115

Designed by
Susan Goans Driggers

GATHER THESE SUPPLIES

Project Surface:
Clay pot, 7"

Paints, Stains, and Finishes:
Acrylic craft paints:
　Porcelain Blue
　Wicker White
Matte spray sealer

Brushes:
Flat brushes, #1, #4, #8

Other Supplies:
Natural sponge
Rub-on transfers: Pansies
Scissors

INSTRUCTIONS

Prepare:
1. See Surface Preparation on page 9. Prepare clay pot.

2. Using a #8 flat brush, basecoat pot with Wicker White.

Sponge the Design:
1. See How to Sponge on page 112. Sponge lower part of pot with Porcelain Blue.

2. Dilute Porcelain Blue paint with water, using 3 parts paint and 1 part water. Using flat brushes, create a painted plaid around the rim of pot with diluted Porcelain Blue.

3. Dip tips of brushes in paint to make vertical stripes of varying widths. Let dry.

4. Paint horizontal stripes around rim, using the same brush technique. Let dry.

Finish:
1. Cut and apply Pansies transfers to pot, following maufacturer's instructions.

2. Apply matte spray sealer.

Relief Design Techniques

Dimensional fabric paints can be used to create designs with raised outlines on pots. The paints come in squeezable bottles that have precision flow tips, making application easy. These paints allows you to apply ultra-thin lines and details in a variety of beautiful colors.

Do not use these pots outdoors. Use them in a sheltered area or indoors to hold kitchen utensils, plants, or as gift containers. Place potted plants in another container and place the container into the decorated pot.

Acrylic craft paints are used to create a whitewash technique over dimensional designs. The technique is simple, and can be done with any color paint. The paints are water-based, so cleanup is simple.

SUPPLIES YOU WILL NEED

Paints, Stains, and Finishes:
Acrylic craft paint
Dimensional paint

Brushes:
Flat brush

Other Supplies:
Cellulose sponge
Disposable plate or palette
Graphite transfer paper
Masking tape
Paper towels
Pen or stylus
Scissors
Tracing paper

HOW TO RELIEF DESIGN

Transfer the Design:
1. Enlarge pattern as directed. Using a pen or stylus, trace pattern on tracing paper. Cut away excess tracing paper from around the design.

2. Tape pattern onto pot, centering the design. Secure top of pattern to top of pot. The tape will act as a hinge.

3. Slide graphite transfer paper under pattern. Secure pattern to pot with more tape.

4. Using a pen or stylus, trace design. Remove tape and pattern, and begin to decorate.

Using Stencils:
1. Tape stencil to pot along top edge of stencil.

2. Trace around inside edges of center portion of stencil design, marking pot with design.

3. Remove tape. Bend stencil down and around right side of pot, keeping design aligned. Use the design part just traced as a guide. Tape stencil in place and trace rest of design.

4. Continue around pot, first to the right then to the left, tracing part of the stencil at a time.

5. Keep tracing until finishing the stencil or reaching the back of the pot. Stop tracing before the two sides of the design meet at the back of the pot. Remove tape and stencil.

Outline the Design:
1. Use dimensional paint to outline the design. Allow the dimensional paint to dry overnight.

Whitewash:
Note: The "whitewash" technique can be done with any color of acrylic paint.

1. On a disposable plate, squeeze out a small amount of acrylic paint. Using a flat brush, pick up a small dab of paint. Blot brush on a paper towel to remove most of the paint.

2. Scrub brush across outlined design on pot to cover a small area with the white paint.

3. Wet a cellulose sponge and squeeze or blot to remove excess water. Immediately wipe sponge across raised painted design to remove the acrylic paint from the raised area.

4. Continue whitewashing design and then wiping paint from raised area, working one section at a time. Whitewash entire design plus a small area outside of the design. If desired, the entire pot can be whitewashed.

TIPS:
• Practice on the bottom of the pot first.

• If too much paint gets in one area, use a terra cotta color paint to mask mistake on the pot.

• To create a weathered look, apply paint to the pot surface and use a natural sponge to wipe off some or most of the paint.

• A second coat of paint can be applied if more color is desired.

• Clean decorated pots with a damp cloth when they become dusty or soiled.

Wild Lace Flowers Pot
Instructions begin on page 119

Seaside Pot
Instructions begin on page 119

Isle of Palms Pot
Instructions begin on page 119

Seaside Pot

Pictured on page 118

Designed by
Cyndi Pfeiffer

GATHER THESE SUPPLIES

Painting Surface:
Clay pot, 6" dia.

Paints, Stains, and Finishes:
Acrylic craft paints:
  Pure Gold
  Raspberry Wine
Dimensional paint:
  Green Haze

Brushes:
Flat scrubber, #8

Other Supplies:
Cellulose sponge
Transfer tool

INSTRUCTIONS

Prepare:
1. See Surface Preparation on page 9. Prepare clay pot.

2. Transfer Seaside Pot Patterns on page 120 to pot.

Paint the Design:
1. Outline design with Green Haze. Let dry overnight.

Finish:
1. See Whitewash on page 117. Using a #8 flat scrubber, whitewash with Raspberry Wine to design.

2. Add accent smudges to shells in design with Pure Gold.

Wild Lace Flowers Pot

Pictured on page 118

Designed by
Cyndi Pfeiffer

GATHER THESE SUPPLIES

Painting Surface:
Clay pot, 9" dia. with handles and feet

Paints, Stains, and Finishes:
Acrylic craft paint:
  Wicker White
Dimensional paint:
  Solid Bronze

Brushes:
Flat scrubber, #8

Other Supplies:
Cellulose sponge
Transfer tool

INSTRUCTIONS

Prepare:
1. See Surface Preparation on page 9. Prepare clay pot.

2. Transfer Wild Lace Flowers Pot Pattern on page 120 to pot.

Paint the Design:
1. Outline design with Solid Bronze. Let dry overnight.

Finish:
1. See Whitewash on page 117. Using a #8 flat scrubber, whitewash with Wicker White.

Isle of Palms Pot

Pictured on page 118

Designed by
Cyndi Pfeiffer

GATHER THESE SUPPLIES

Painting Surface:
Clay pot, 8" dia.

Paints, Stains, and Finishes:
Acrylic craft paint:
  Victorian Rose
Dimensional paint:
  Garnet Red Pearl

Brushes:
Flat scrubber, #8

Other Supplies:
Cellulose sponge
Transfer tool

INSTRUCTIONS

Prepare:
1. See Surface Preparation on page 9. Prepare clay pot.

2. Transfer Isle of Palms Pot Pattern on page 120 to pot.

Paint the Design:
1. Outline design with Garnet Red Pearl. Let dry overnight.

Finish:
1. See Whitewash on page 117. Using a #8 flat scrubber, whitewash with Victorian Rose.

Seaside Pot Patterns

Enlarge patterns 135%

Wild Lace Flowers Pot Pattern

Enlarge pattern 135%

Isle of Palms Pot Pattern

Enlarge pattern 135%

**Rope &
Tassel Pot**
Instructions begin
on page 122

Classic Shell Pot
Instructions begin
on page 122

**Sweet
Marinda
Angel Pot**
Instructions begin
on page 122

Rope & Tassel Pot

Pictured on page 121

Designed by
Cyndi Pfeiffer

GATHER THESE SUPPLIES

Painting Surface:
Clay pot, 11" dia.

Paints, Stains, and Finishes:
Acrylic craft paint:
 Wicker White
Dimensional paint:
 Copper

Brushes:
Flat scrubber, #8

Other Supplies:
Cellulose sponge
Stencils:
 Rope & Tassel
 Village Vine
Transfer tool

INSTRUCTIONS

Prepare:
1. See Surface Preparation on page 9. Prepare clay pot.

2. Transfer Rope & Tassel stencil around pot below rim, using photo on page 121 as a guide.

3. Transfer rope design to make border at top and bottom edges of pot.

4. Transfer Village Vine stencil to make borders around rim and bottom of pot.

Paint the Design:
1. Outline design with Copper. Let dry overnight.

Finish:
1. See Whitewash on page 117. Using a #8 flat scrubber, whitewash with Wicker White.

Classic Shell Pot

Pictured on page 121

Designed by
Cyndi Pfeiffer

GATHER THESE SUPPLIES

Project Surface:
Clay pot, 11" dia.

Paints, Stains, and Finishes:
Acrylic craft paint:
 Wicker White
Dimensional paint:
 Brown

Brushes:
Flat scrubber, #8

Other Supplies:
Cellulose sponge
Transfer tool

INSTRUCTIONS

Prepare:
1. See Surface Preparation on page 9. Prepare clay pot.

2. Transfer Classic Shell Pot Pattern on page 123 to pot.

Paint the Design:
1. Outline design with Brown. Let dry overnight.

Finish:
1. See Whitewash on page 117. Using a #8 flat scrubber, whitewash with Wicker White.

Sweet Marinda Angel Pot

Pictured on page 121

Designed by
Cyndi Pfeiffer

GATHER THESE SUPPLIES

Painting Surface:
Clay pot, 7" dia.

Paints, Stains, and Finishes:
Acrylic craft paint:
 Wicker White
Dimensional paint:
 Solid Bronze

Brushes:
Flat scrubber, #8

Other Supplies:
Cellulose sponge
Transfer tool

INSTRUCTIONS

Prepare:
1. See Surface Preparation on page 9. Prepare clay pot.

2. Transfer Sweet Marinda Angel Pot Pattern on page 123 to pot.

Paint the Design:
1. Outline design with Solid Bronze. Let dry overnight.

Finish:
1. See Whitewash on page 117. Using a #8 flat scrubber, whitewash with Wicker White.

Classic Shell Pot Pattern

Enlarge pattern 175%

Sweet Marinda Angel Pot Pattern

Enlarge pattern 135%

Product Sources

Plaid Enterprises, Inc., Norcross, GA, produces high quality paint products that are formulated for decorative painting. Following are the product names and numbers:

FolkArt® Acrylic Colors:

401 True Blue
402 Light Blue
403 Navy Blue
404 Periwinkle
405 Teal
406 Hunter Green
407 Kelly Green
408 Green
410 Lavender
411 Purple
412 Magenta
413 Pink
414 Cardinal Red
415 Maroon
416 Dark Brown
417 Teddy Bear Brown
418 Buckskin Brown
419 Teddy Bear Tan
420 Linen
421 Portrait Light
422 Portrait Medium
424 Light Gray
425 Medium Gray
426 Dark Gray
427 Ivory White
428 Rose White
429 Winter White
430 Spring White
431 French Vanilla
432 Sunflower
433 Terra Cotta
434 Berry Wine
435 Napthol Crimson
436 Engine Red
437 Lipstick
438 Ballet Pink
439 Purple Lilac
440 Violet Pansy
441 Sterling Blue
442 Baby Blue

443 Night Sky
444 Patina
445 Mint Green
447 Leaf Green
448 Green Forest
449 Olive Green
450 Parchment
451 Cappuccino
452 Raw Sienna
455 Medium Yellow
456 True Burgundy
457 Ice Blue
459 Hauser Light Green
460 Hauser Medium Green
461 Hauser Dark Green
462 Burnt Umber
463 Dioxide Purple
464 Cerulean Blue
465 Sky Blue
466 Bright Pastel Green
467 Italian Sage
468 Gray Plum
469 Dark Plum
470 Lime Light
471 Green Umber
472 Mushroom
475 Gray Green
476 Asphaltum
477 Payne's Gray
478 Lime Yellow
479 Pure Black
480 Titanium White
481 Aqua
484 Brilliant Ultramarine
485 Raw Umber
486 Prussian Blue
601 Clay Bisque
602 Country Twill
607 Settlers Blue
608 Heartland Blue
609 Thunder Blue
611 Barnyard Red
612 Holiday Red
613 Charcoal Grey
614 Buttercream
615 Georgia Peach
617 Peach Perfection
619 Poetry Green

620 Victorian Rose
624 Potpourri Rose
625 Lavender Sachet
627 Tangerine
628 Pure Orange
629 Red Light
630 Poppy Red
632 Rose Pink
633 Baby Pink
634 Hot Pink
635 Fuchsia
636 Red Violet
637 Orchid
638 Purple Passion
639 French Blue
640 Light Periwinkle
641 Brilliant Blue
642 Blue Ink
643 Azure Blue
644 Grass Green
645 Basil Green
646 Aspen Green
647 Emerald Isle
649 Warm White
679 Turner's Yellow
682 Bright Peach
683 Orange Light
684 Medium Orange
685 Bright Pink
686 Burnt Carmine
688 Light Fuschia
689 Pure Magenta
701 Icy White
702 Gray Mist
704 Milkshake
705 Almond Parfait
708 Dove Gray
711 Bluebonnet
713 Coastal Blue
715 Amish Blue
719 Blue Ribbon
720 Cobalt Blue
721 Denim Blue
723 Mystic Green
724 Evergreen
725 Tartan Green
726 Green Meadow
730 Southern Pine

733 Teal Green
735 Lemon Custard
736 School Bus Yellow
737 Buttercrunch
738 Peach Cobbler
741 Glazed Carrots
745 Huckleberry
747 Salmon
751 Strawberry Parfait
752 Berries 'n Cream
753 Rose Chiffon
754 Rose Garden
758 Alzarian Crimson
759 Whipped Berry
761 Plum Chiffon
765 Porcelain Blue
767 Spring Rose
901 Wicker White
902 Taffy
903 Tapioca
904 Lemonade
905 Buttercup
906 Summer Sky
908 Indigo
909 Bluebell
910 Slate Blue
912 Promenade Coral
913 Cinnamon
914 Light Red Oxide
917 Yellow Ochre
918 Yellow Light
920 Autumn Leaves
922 Bayberry
923 Clover
924 Thicket
925 Wrought Iron
926 Shamrock
927 Old Ivy
929 Cotton Candy
930 Primrose
932 Calico Red
933 Heather
934 Plum Pudding
935 Raspberry Wine
936 Barn Wood
937 Dapple Gray
938 Licorice
939 Butter Pecan
940 Coffee Bean
941 Acorn Brown
942 Honeycomb
943 Burnt Sienna

944 Nutmeg
945 Maple Syrup
949 Skintone
951 Apple Spice
953 Camel
954 Fresh Foliage
955 Sweetheart Pink
957 Burgundy
958 Christmas Red
959 English Mustard
961 Turquoise
962 Wintergreen
964 Midnight
966 Raspberry Sherbet

FolkArt® Metallic Colors:
651 Blue Topaz
652 Rose Shimmer
653 Emerald Green
654 Amethyst
655 Aquamarine
656 Blue Sapphire
657 Regal Red
658 Antique Gold
659 Pearl White
660 Pure Gold
661 Sequin Black
662 Silver Sterling
663 Solid Bronze
664 Copper
665 Garnet Red
666 Antique Copper
667 Gunmetal Gray
668 Plum
669 Periwinkle
670 Blue Pearl
671 Peridot
672 Mint Pearl
673 Rose Pearl
674 Peach Pearl
675 Champagne
676 Inca Gold

Apple Barrel® Gloss
Enamel Colors:
20351 Real Burgundy
20352 Real Denim
20353 Real Navy
20354 Real Brown
20355 Terra Cotta
20356 Lavender
20357 Patina

20621 White
20622 Eggshell
20623 Antique White
20624 Dolphin Gray
20625 Deep Purple
20627 Purple Velvet
20629 Raspberry
20631 Pink Blush
20632 Holiday Rose
20633 Cranberry Red
20634 Rose Wine
20636 Real Red
20637 Hot Rod Red
20639 Tangerine
20643 Bermuda Beach
20645 Real Yellow
20646 Dandelion Yellow
20647 Crown Gold
20648 Mossy Green
20649 Forest Green
20651 Real Green
20652 Bayberry
20653 Arbor Green
20656 Lanier Blue
20657 Pinwheel Blue
20660 Real Blue
20661 Goodnight Blue
20662 Black
20663 Beachcomber Beige
20665 Mocha
20666 Coffee Bean

Plaster Paints:
67501 White
67502 Cream
67503 Beige
67504 Yellow
67505 Mustard
67506 Pale Peach
67507 Orange
67508 Red
67509 Country Burgundy
67510 Petal Pink
67511 Lavender
67512 Deep Purple
67513 True Blue
67514 Country Blue
67515 Powder Blue
67516 Christmas Green
67517 Hunter Green
67518 Teddy Bear Brown
67519 Fudge Brown

67520 Gray
67521 Black
67522 Gold
67523 Silver
67529 Pale Yellow
67530 Coral
67531 Mauve
67532 Baby Pink
67533 Periwinkle
67534 Teal
67535 Sage
67536 Terra Cotta
67537 Cocoa
67538 Ivy

FolkArt® Painting Mediums:
Crackle Medium #694
Extender #947
Glazing Medium #893

FolkArt® Finishes:
Acrylic Spray Sealer #788
Waterbase Varnish #791

Stencil Decor® Products:
Precut stencils
Dry brush stencil paints
Paint crayons
Stencil brushes

Simply® Stencil Designs:
Following are the designs used in this book:
Autumn Leaves #28350
Backyard Birdhouse #28764
Cut Your Own Blank #28584
Ribbon & Bow #29007
Rope & Tassel #28905
Village Vine #28440

Dry Brush Paints (first number listed), and **Paint Crayons** (second number listed):
Cameo Peach #26201, #26533
Turtle Dove Gray
#26202, #26534
Vintage Burgundy
#26203, #26535
Promenade Rose
#26204, #26536
Tea Time Rose
#26205, #26537

Truffles Brown
#26206, #26538
Ship's Fleet Navy
#26207, #26539
Herb Garden Green
#26208, #26540
Sherwood Forest
#26209, #26541
Wild Ivy Green
#26210, #26542
Ol' Pioneer Red
#26211, #26543
Cherries in the Snow
#26212, #26544
Romantic Rose
#26213, #26545
Blue Chintz #26214, #26546
Wildflower Honey
#26214, #26547
Ecru Lace #26215, #26548
English Lavender
#26216, #26549
Sunny Brook Yellow
#26218, #26550
White Linen #26219, #26551
Dusty Rose #26220, #26560
Bouquet Pink #26221, #26561
Quilt Blue #26222, #26569
Vanity Teal #26223, #26570
Andiron Black
#26224, #26574
Eggplant #26225, # 26580
Hunter Green #26226, #26581
Maroon #26227, #26582
Indigo Blue #26228, #26583
Sage Green #26229, #26584
Periwinkle #26230, #26585
China Blue #26231, #26586
True Blue #26232, #26587

Stencil Gels:
26101 White
26102 Ivory Lace
26103 Lemon Peel
26104 Daffodil Yellow
26105 Adobe Sand
26106 French Vanilla
26107 Pumpkin
26108 Poppy Red
26109 Pink Blush
26110 Wood
26111 Ruby Red

26112 Grape
26113 Light Amethyst
26114 Deep Purple
26115 Dark Sapphire
26116 Wedgwood Blue
26117 Tempest Blue
26118 Blue Blazer
26119 Teal
26120 Spanish Moss
26121 Forest Shade
26122 Village Green
26123 Fern
26124 Juniper
26125 Cactus
26126 Wild Ivy
26127 Taupe
27128 Twig
27129 Russet
27130 Black
27131 Shadow Gray
27132 King's Gold

Faster Plaster™
Plaster products by Plaid Enterprises, Inc., make available a wide range of plaster molds, plaster paints, and a high-quality dry plaster. The following plaster molds were used in this book:

Molds:
Bunny Patch Picks #67122
Spring Garden Picks #67121

Decorator Blocks®
Special foam printing blocks and paints are available from Plaid Enterprises, Inc., in a variety of designs and colors. The following designs and colors were used in this book:

Designs:
Critters #53220
Cut Your Own Blank #53226
Grape Vine #53203
Little Garden Flowers #53219
Mini Fruits #53422
Tulips #53213

Metric Conversion Chart

MM-Millimetres   CM-Centimetres

INCHES TO MILLIMETRES AND CENTIMETRES

INCHES	MM	CM	INCHES	CM	INCHES	CM
⅛	3	0.3	9	22.9	30	76.2
¼	6	0.6	10	25.4	31	78.7
½	13	1.3	12	30.5	33	83.8
⅝	16	1.6	13	33.0	34	86.4
¾	19	1.9	14	35.6	35	88.9
⅞	22	2.2	15	38.1	36	91.4
1	25	2.5	16	40.6	37	94.0
1¼	32	3.2	17	43.2	38	96.5
1½	38	3.8	18	45.7	39	99.1
1¾	44	4.4	19	48.3	40	101.6
2	51	5.1	20	50.8	41	104.1
2½	64	6.4	21	53.3	42	106.7
3	76	7.6	22	55.9	43	109.2
3½	89	8.9	23	58.4	44	111.8
4	102	10.2	24	61.0	45	114.3
4½	114	11.4	25	63.5	46	116.8
5	127	12.7	26	66.0	47	119.4
6	152	15.2	27	68.6	48	121.9
7	178	17.8	28	71.1	49	124.5
8	203	20.3	29	73.7	50	127.0

YARDS TO METRES

YARDS	METRES	YARDS	METRES	YARDS	METRES	YARDS	METRES	YARDS	METRES
⅛	0.11	2⅛	1.94	4⅛	3.77	6⅛	5.60	8⅛	7.43
¼	0.23	2¼	2.06	4¼	3.89	6¼	5.72	8¼	7.54
⅜	0.34	2⅜	2.17	4⅜	4.00	6⅜	5.83	8⅜	7.66
½	0.46	2½	2.29	4½	4.11	6½	5.94	8½	7.77
⅝	0.57	2⅝	2.40	4⅝	4.23	6⅝	6.06	8⅝	7.89
¾	0.69	2¾	2.51	4¾	4.34	6¾	6.17	8¾	8.00
⅞	0.80	2⅞	2.63	4⅞	4.46	6⅞	6.29	8⅞	8.12
1	0.91	3	2.74	5	4.57	7	6.40	9	8.23
1⅛	1.03	3⅛	2.86	5⅛	4.69	7⅛	6.52	9⅛	8.34
1¼	1.14	3¼	2.97	5¼	4.80	7¼	6.63	9¼	8.46
1⅜	1.26	3⅜	3.09	5⅜	4.91	7⅜	6.74	9⅜	8.57
1½	1.37	3½	3.20	5½	5.03	7½	6.86	9½	8.69
1⅝	1.49	3⅝	3.31	5⅝	5.14	7⅝	6.97	9⅝	8.80
1¾	1.60	3¾	3.43	5¾	5.26	7¾	7.09	9¾	8.92
1⅞	1.71	3⅞	3.54	5⅞	5.37	7⅞	7.20	9⅞	9.03
2	1.83	4	3.66	6	5.49	8	7.32	10	9.14

Index